Discovering God as Companion

Past Issues of What Canst Thou Say?

Why Canst Thou Say? Is a newsletter in which Quakers share first-hand their mystical experiences and contemplative practice. The first fourteen issues were published from October 1994 through May 1997. Each issue featured a variety of topics. Beginning with issue 15 in August 1997, the publication became quarterly, with each issue focusing on a specific theme:

To subscribe or purchase copies of back issues of *What Canst Thou Say?,* see <whatcanstthousay.org> or write to WCTS, 1035 Hereford Drive, Blue Bell PA 19422-1925.

Discovering God as Companion

Real Life Stories from *What Canst Thou Say?*

Mariellen Gilpin, Editor

Discovering God as Companion
Real Life Stories from *What Canst Thou Say?*
Mariellen Gilpin, Editor

For information on this book or the publication *What Canst Thou Say?* contact:

What Canst Thou Say?
1035 Hereford Drive
Blue Bell PA 19422-1925
<http://www.whatcanstthousay.org>

Published by AuthorHouse
1663 Liberty Drive, Suite 200
Bloomington, IN 47403
<http://www.authorhouse.com>

First published by AuthorHouse 2/23/07

ISBN: 978-1-4259-8770-1 (sc)

Printed in the United States of America
Bloomington, Indiana

This book is printed on acid-free paper.

Contents

God in Times of Pain and Despair 60

Afterword: God as Companion 145

Appendices

Acknowledgments

The stories in this book were first published in a newsletter, *What Canst Thou Say?* (WCTS). WCTS was begun as a quarterly newsletter in 1994 by Jean Roberts and Jim Flory to encourage sharing of mystical experience and contemplative practice among Quakers. They wrote, "It is like launching a kite: Jean and Jim will run down the beach to get it airborne, but lacking the breeze of your contributions of articles, responses, questions and quotes, it will not fly."

In the years since, Lissa Field, Mariellen Gilpin, Kathryn Gordon, Lieselotte Heil, Richard Himmer, Chris Johns, Sue Kern, Linda Lee, Judy Lumb, Marcelle Martin, Patricia McBee, Grayce Mesner, Roena Oesting, Amy Perry, Carol Roth, Morgan Roth, Kathy Tapp, Eleanor Warnock, Margaret Willits, and Wayne Yarnall have helped publish WCTS. All have been volunteers. Special thanks, too, to all whose articles, responses, questions and quotes have given vitality to the ongoing publication of *What Canst Thou Say?*.

Special thanks go to Kathy Tapp, Eleanor Warnock and Patricia McBee for their editorial comments and suggestions, and to Judy Lumb for going many extra miles to shepherd this book to publication. Steve Clapp and Ellen Michaud have shared expertise and encouragement. Dorothy Neumann, Barbara Kessel, and Carol Roth read and commented on early drafts. Linda Lee kept in good countenance while searching for the sources of the historical quotations. Martha Turner helped with book promotion. The members and attenders of Urbana-Champaign Friends Meeting, Illinois, have enthusiastically supported the whole enterprise. My husband John Gilpin's constancy in love has taught me what to expect of God, who first exhibited that quality and taught us to hope for it.

Mariellen Gilpin, Editor

Introduction

Discovering God as Companion is a collection of stories of mystical openings among modern people, most of them members of the Religious Society of Friends (Quakers). Writers share their stories because they have a deep sense of spiritual responsibility. They have hungered and been filled, and they are eager to share their knowledge that *God is*.

Many spiritual traditions caution about the difficulties and dangers of trying to teach or even communicate about mystical experiences. The world's great spiritual literature warns about making much of one's mystical experience. But in our modern rationalist culture the mystical is often thought to be a mental aberration. Seldom does the word get out that the mystic is a sturdy worker in God's vineyard: 16th century mystic Teresa of Avila not only founded but administered an order of nuns, mixing the mystical with great practical good sense. As Dorothee Soelle wrote,

Mysticism is the experience of the oneness and wholeness of life. Therefore, mysticism's perception of life, its vision, is also the unrelenting perception of how fragmented life is. Suffering on account of that fragmentation and finding it unbearable is part of mysticism. Finding God fragmented into rich and poor, top and bottom, sick and well, weak and mighty: that's the mystic's suffering. The resistance of Saint Francis or Elisabeth of Thuringia or of Martin Luther King, Jr,. grew out of the perception of beauty. And the longest lasting and most dangerous resistance is the one that was born from beauty.[1]

The writers in this book—of whom I am one—have yearned to tell our stories of what God has done for us. Our stories are too important to hug to ourselves forever. Someone else needs the comfort and reassurance and challenge these stories provide. We were helped to overcome an obstacle, and someone may be helped by our stories. Someone is searching as we have sought, just as forlorn and despairing as we were, and we want our readers to know which rock to look under for the answer. God is not one size fits all; we can't depend on learning one prayer and reading one book and having all our problems fall into line like little robots. God has provided help uniquely designed for our special needs, and our writers want others to know God will honor their individuality as well. In "Tractor Dream" Lynda Schaller's hunger for God is awakened when she dreams about her father's tractor; in "Healing Old Wounds" a wooden mouse on a cheeseboard helps heal Judith Weir's troubled relationship with her ex-husband.

To tell our stories is to honor God. But the experience of God's presence is intimate; it cannot be described in words. Words are inadequate, and people who have not had our experience won't understand. They may be scared, or judgmental, or stop listening. Thus, mystics don't always share what they have experienced. On the other hand, there is a great longing to share with others who have had like experiences. And we want to be companions for those others.

Many of the writers in *Discovering God as Companion* have been helped by hearing others' stories, and many of us have decided to share our own stories. We have learned we are not crazy, and we can tap into a body of experience. Together we can ground our experiences and better understand them, and help others ground themselves as well. Isolation is disorienting, but when we meet others we learn we are not alone. Together we can find wholeness.

Some spiritual traditions warn against trying to write down the things of God, for fear of putting a strait jacket on our understanding of the Spirit of God. We must not tell people precisely what to expect of God, because God is Creativity Itself—we can't pour God into any mold. The way God moves in my life is unique to my needs, my situation, my personality. In "The Price of Professionalism" public defender Steven Gross awakens to God when a murderer grieves her murdered partner.

Stories are the spiritual heart of the Bible. Stories tell how God acted in one life, dealing with one person. We may laugh at Abraham working the wiles of a horse trader on the Creator of the Universe, but we realize that although God was dealing with a horse trader, he didn't hesitate to communicate with Abraham. Abraham was changed by his encounter. God has communicated with me, with my limitations and maladjustments. When I tell how I have changed as a result of that communication, maybe you will feel emboldened to listen for God in a new way. Your experience will be unique to you. Someone else's story may point toward God, but when you find God, it will be in your own way. Marti Matthews finds God in the act of flossing her teeth; in "Reflections on Living Reverently" Marlou Carlson longs to be always centered in God, choosing less busyness and more listening.

The stories in this book were published in *What Canst Thou Say?* between 1994 and 2004. The biographical sketches are presented as originally published. The stories are grouped under five themes:

God Breaking In—When times seem the most ordinary, we can be amazed, challenged, inspired by God's abounding and abiding great love.

God in Nature—We can be restored and nourished by discovering God's creation and our oneness with that creation.

God in Times of Pain and Despair—When times are the most painful, we can be carried by insight, guidance, and a sense of God's presence and grace.

Living Faithfully—When we are filled with love for God, we can be called to serve God in deep and wondrous ways.

In Celebration—When God is intimate friend and companion, all of life—painful, ordinary, marvelous—is rich and full of joy.

There is a deep honesty—a deep sharing—in these stories offered by ordinary people who are authentic lovers of God. In this book you will meet a God who is alive and well, and still in the business of changing lives. To read these stories is to open oneself to being changed. Enjoy!

God Breaking In

Suddenly I felt the walls between visible and invisible grow thin and the eternal seemed to break through into the world where I was. I saw no flood of light; I heard no voice, but I felt as though I were face to face with a higher order of reality than that of the trees or mountains. ...A sense of mission broke in on me and I felt I was being called to a well-defined task of life to which I then and there dedicated myself. I was brought to a new level of life and have never quite lost the transforming effect of the experience.[2]

—Rufus Jones (1863–1948)

(*What Canst Thou Say?* November 2000 "Visions and Voices")

~ ~ ~ ~ ~ ~ ~ ~ ~ ~ ~ ~ ~

In the most ordinary of times, we can be challenged and inspired by intimations of God's abounding and abiding great love. Stephen Angell is going about his business when God asks him to deliver a message to Camp David—and gives him directions for driving there. In "A Dream" Wayne Swanger awakens to find himself in the presence of God. Ray Bentman, in "Transformed by the Spirit," senses God's presence in a Friends Meeting for Business.

God breaking in can result in shaking, inner light, voices, visions, knowings, or a sense of presence. In "An Absolute Total Knowing" Jennifer Frick knows, in a surprisingly physical way, that her mother-in-law is going to die. In "New Eyes" Connie Lezenby has a series of visions, and comes to see God in a new light.

The mighty power of God can change our concept of reality; the eternal may break into the now. Feelings of ultimate love, amazing transformations, comforting voices, and calls to service may happen at any time. In "The Nominating Voice" Elizabeth Meyer is washing dishes when she is called to preside over her Quaker meeting. Theodora E. Waring is given the gift of speaking in tongues in a dormitory restroom ("Baptism of the Holy Spirit"). In "A Numinous Presence" a friend's prayer at her dying husband's bedside ushers in a sense of God's loving presence for Alison Lohans.

In an interview, Elaine Emily reminds us that intense experiences of God may leave one disoriented, and mystical experiences may shake out trauma memories long buried. Those memories need to be brought into the light so the person can heal. Good therapy can help, but good spiritual guidance is also necessary. God is not finished with us yet! God has work for us to do, and integrating the old trauma is the beginning of the work, not the end.

Spirituality in the body, which can cause shaking and other symptoms, is known in mystical traditions around the world. In the Hindu literature, dramatic spiritual energy is called Kundalini. What relevance does a Hindu word have for the western world? Kathy Tapp in "Salt Doll" finds that the Kundalini tradition helps her understand and live constructively with the energy, when the wisdom of the western cultures did not help her. In "Giving Birth to the Sun" Marcelle Martin also shares the help she has received from eastern traditions.

Special dispensations bring with them special responsibilities. Ecstasies require commitment to work in God's vineyard. We can all draw courage and sustenance from the stories these writers relate.

~~~~~~~~~~~~~~

Go to Camp David

Stephen L. Angell

In June of 1970, I was clerk of the General Committee of Friends Committee on National Legislation (FCNL). President Nixon was in office. It was a time of great national unrest over the Vietnam War. On this particular weekend, I was traveling from my home in New York State to Washington, D.C., to attend a meeting of the FCNL Executive Committee. It also happened to be the weekend of the largest anti-Vietnam War demonstration, which took place just following the killing of four Kent State University students. I had appointments in Washington in connection with my consulting business; it required precise planning of my travel time.

Before I left for Washington, a Friend called who urgently wanted to tell me some Quakers and others would gather in Lafayette Park, opposite the White House, to hold Richard Nixon in the Light. My friend hoped I could attend. I said I would if I could.

For a reason I did not know, the route to Washington was not the one I would ordinarily have taken. While traveling, I listened to my car radio. Much of the news was about the national unrest, the aftermath of the Kent State killings, the upcoming demonstration, and a report that the President was at Camp David. I was focused on getting to Washington for my appointment. All seemed to be going well.

I got a message: *Go to Camp David and give a message to the President.* This took me completely by surprise, since I had had no previous thought of doing anything like this. First of all, I had no notion how to get to Camp David, and secondly I did not know what message I should give to the President. This had to be a whole lot of nonsense, I thought, and I was right on time to meet my personal commitments. I kept trying to put this out of my mind, but it would not let me go.

I kept driving and found myself in the Catoctin Mountains. I came to a side road that veered to the right off the main highway and received the instruction I should turn there. I had no notion where it led. Besides, I was right on schedule and did not know if Camp David was 10, 25, 50 miles away. It made no sense to turn there, and I refused to do it. I drove on down the highway for about two miles, and I literally could not drive any further. I had to pull the car over to the side of the road. This requires another story:

A few months earlier, I had heard over the radio that on a given date Norman Vincent Peale, a spiritual advisor to Richard Nixon, was going to have open office hours at his church in New York City, and anyone who wanted to come in and talk to him could do so. I got a message then that I should talk to Dr. Peale about his support of President Nixon and the war in Vietnam. I had tried to put this out of my mind as something I did not want to do. However, on the day these office hours were to occur, I was in New York City, and I had no conflicting appointments and could easily have gone to see Dr. Peale—but I refused. This left me so uncomfortable I finally said, "Please let me go this time, I *promise* if you ever again ask me to do something like this, I will do it." *This was the next time!*

I turned my car around and went back. A short way down the road was a billboard advertising an orchard and I thought, "Good. I will end up in someone's orchard and I can turn around, forget this nonsense and go on my way." The road, however, went through the orchard and came to an intersection. I said, "O.K. you're in charge; which way do I go?" The instruction was to turn left.

I then began to think, "Well, if I am supposed to go to Camp David, maybe I should stop and ask." But then I thought, "No, if I am supposed to get there, I will." I continued down the road and came to Catoctin National Park. The instruction was to turn into the park. There was a park office there where I thought I could ask my way, but my answer to myself was again, "No, if I am supposed to get there I will." I traveled into the park, rounded a curve and saw a sign: Camp David. I had to pull over to the side of the road and regain my composure.

Well, now I was at Camp David. I had to do it. I thought, "They will think I am crazy if I tell them I have a message for the President but I don't know what it is." I pulled up to the gatehouse. There were two officers inside. One officer asked me my business, and I said I had come with a message for the President. He said if I gave it to him he would see that the President received it. I said that I could not give him the message but I could only tell him how I got there and started to tell my story. While I was talking to the one officer, the other one was on the telephone. He finally came over and spoke to the officer listening to me. He then told me if I would pull my car off to the side, one of the president's staff would come out and speak with me. I did this; shortly a man came from inside the compound and sat down in the passenger seat of my car.

I related my story of how I got to Camp David, and then reached the point of relating a message—which until that moment I had no notion of. I had faith that when the time came the words would be there. My feelings and opinions about Richard Nixon were very negative. I have no clear recollection of what my exact words were. But all of a sudden I had a great sense of compassion for the man. My words conveyed this by acknowledging the great weight and concern he must be under for the state of the country and the difficult decisions he must make.

I went on to say that on Sunday at 11:00 AM Quakers and others would be holding a Meeting for Worship in Lafayette Park to pray for him, that he might be well guided in the decisions that he had to make. I said that we would welcome him among us; however, we would understand if he could not be there, but hoped that he might worship with us from inside the White House.

The presidential staff person wanted information about me. The most recent issue of the FCNL Newsletter had my picture and an accompanying article. I reached into my attaché case on the back seat; there on top of a pile of papers was the publication. I handed this to him and he left. I resumed my trip to Washington.

The President did not attend the meeting in Lafayette Park. I did, however, write him a letter expressing our regret that he could not be with us. The compassionate feelings that came over me while at Camp David were still with me. A week or so later I received a three- or four-sentence letter of appreciation signed by Richard Nixon. It appeared to be authentic.

The impact of this experience has shaped my life, because I know experientially that there is a power well beyond my comprehension that can give direction to my life. While I have had no repeat experiences as dramatic as this one, I have clearly experienced times when the direction for my life came from outside myself.

Stephen L. Angell is a member of Kendall Friends Meeting (Pennsylvania). He has been involved with Alternatives to Violence since 1975. He has done extensive work in prisons and in conflict areas around the world.

(*What Canst Thou Say?* November 2000, "Visions and Voices")

~~~~~~~~~~~~~~

An Absolute Total Knowing

Jennifer Frick

When I entered Saint Mary's that morning in January of 1995, the church was empty and still. A few candles flickered in front of the statue of Mary. I had come to light a candle and pray for my mother-in-law, Barb, during her bypass surgery. I had told Barb just the night before that I had lit a candle and prayed for her, and that I would go back to the church and do the same the next day while she was in surgery. Although I was a Quaker, my in-laws were Catholics, and I knew going to Saint Mary's and lighting a candle would mean something special to Barb.

I had just begun to pray when I was startled by an overwhelming sensation that seemed to come from outside me. The feeling flooded through me, filled my chest and flowed down through my arms. I could not explain or ignore it. I opened my eyes and looked around. I stood up. I shook my arms and swung them about. I paced up and down the aisles of the church, but the feeling would not go away. It neither lessened nor changed, and did not fade until several hours after I left Saint Mary's.

There were no definite words, no voices ringing through the church or whispering in my ear. There was only this—absolute and total knowing: *She's not going to make it through this.* Yet, that she would die didn't seem likely. She'd had so many tests to see if she was strong enough for surgery. All of the doctors were certain she would be fine. And yet I knew. I knew as I had never known anything before.

She was scheduled to go into surgery at 8:30 Friday morning. A hundred little things caused me to run late, and I didn't get to the church until a couple of hours later. I was so late I almost didn't go. I found out later she had gone into surgery late, and was still being operated on while I was praying for her.

I waited until I knew my husband Bill would be back at his parents' house to feed their Irish setter before I called. "She was fine," he said. "The doctors were pleased."

I thought, "Should I say something? Should I tell him what happened in the church?"

I told him, and we planned that I would stay with my father-in-law. I didn't know what I could do; I just knew I didn't want him to be alone when his wife died. Monday passed uneventfully. The bypass surgery had worked; her toes were pink. I thought, "What had the message meant?"

Barb was a heavy smoker, and her lungs were not good. On Tuesday the doctors put in a breathing tube. It was very uncomfortable, and they sedated her.

She suffered a massive stroke. Half her brain was destroyed. On Friday, my father-in-law made the decision to turn off the machines. The doctors predicted she would last only a few hours, but he said, "She's a fighter," and he was right. She died Monday.

Why had I received this warning? My son David had died at birth a little over a year before, and I had received no such warning then. There were things I could have done to prevent David's death. It didn't seem fair. Why had I been warned about Barb but not David? It didn't make sense. I could do nothing for Barb, and yet I knew. But because I knew, I stayed with my father-in-law, and he was not alone.

I do not believe in predestination, and knowing something before it happens conflicts with my theology. And yet, in the end, there is only this: I knew.

Jennifer Frick reports that she can't get clear to pray for anything else, or center, until she has prayed for others. She is a member of West Richmond Friends Meeting (Indiana) and a graduate of Christian Theological Seminary.

(*What Canst Thou Say?* August 2004 "Knowings")

~ ~ ~ ~ ~ ~ ~ ~ ~ ~ ~

Listen! I will unfold a mystery; we shall not all die, but we shall all be changed in a flash, in a twinkling of an eye. —Corinthians 15:51–53

(*What Canst Thou Say?* November 2001 "Kundalini Energy")

~ ~ ~ ~ ~ ~ ~ ~ ~ ~ ~

Voices and Visions

James Baker

There is a holy Other which I have come to call the Presence, closer than the marrow of my bones, which can speak with a voice, vision, dream, illuminating the solitude at the center of my being. This Innerness and I have an ongoing conversation—a voice, yet not a voice, yet a voice—speaking from the Silence, like a Light that I discover new each day, becoming very quiet if I stray off my path. In my life this communication must come first, must be primal, must take precedence or I lose my way. Such things are private and sacred. To speak of these things seems to me to be as inappropriate as if one were to take the clothes off one's beloved in public and say, "See how beautiful she is." It is not given to be talked about—only in very rare circumstances. One does not throw pearls indiscriminately.

What Canst Thou Say? November 2000 "Visions and Voices")

~ ~ ~ ~ ~ ~ ~ ~ ~ ~ ~ ~ ~

Baptism of the Holy Spirit

Theodora E. Waring

In February 1962 my daughter Kitty Waring, a junior at Earlham College, sounded a bit blue, so I went out to visit. We decided to attend Clear Creek Friends Meeting's potluck supper. Afterward, we walked in the nearby cemetery. Kitty had something she wanted to tell me. She used the metaphor of the path we were traversing. "See, Mom, look behind us, the path we are on has turned a corner. I feel as if my life has, too. I have been baptized in the Holy Spirit."

I knew nothing of that term, so I asked intellectual questions. I was still puzzled when we went to bed. The next day she suggested I talk with two or three Earlham professors whose lives had been turned around by their baptism of the Holy Spirit. I did, including one venerable professor whose Quaker roots went back to Philadelphia, which made me feel I could accept his story. He spoke of the Holy Spirit often filling him up after periods of emptiness in his life.

Kitty and two friends took me out to supper the next day and tried to explain how their lives were consumed with a new devotion to Christ since receiving the baptism of the Holy Spirit. I plied them with rational questions, which did nothing to help me understand. Sunday evening when Kitty was at the library, I sat in her dorm room and talked to God. I acknowledged I had told my children to pray to God, but frankly my prayer life wasn't real for me. These people who were baptized with the Holy Spirit had something far better.

I sensed I was being offered an opportunity to come closer to God. I did not know what it would mean in my life, but I was willing to walk in faith and step out. I knew my Quaker conscience would not let me use any language unfamiliar to me. We don't talk about baptism because we don't follow that sacrament; we don't talk about the Holy Spirit much but do talk about the Spirit within. The only words I could think of were "Here I am, God. Will your Holy Spirit get in touch with my spirit?" I felt I had made a tremendous commitment, with no idea how it would impact my life. I felt like Chicken Little, expecting the sky to fall down imminently.

When Kitty returned from the library I told her in a very embarrassed manner that I had committed myself to God. She was thrilled and rushed off to tell her friends who gathered around, laid their hands on me, prayed in tongues and assured me I had been baptized in the Holy Spirit. I knew I would never do anything as unusual as speak in tongues. They told me to ask for a sign from God. I inwardly asked that my husband Tom would accept whatever was happening to me and not ridicule it. That night I spoke in tongues in my dream.

The next two days I felt as if I were filled with effervescent champagne, a bubbling over of new life. I went to the library to find a Bible. I had a new hunger for the Bible and God's Word. I slept soundly, ate ravenously, and leapt across campus. I felt renewed in a mysterious way. For the first time I became aware of a deep spiritual thirst.

Then the day came for me to fly back to Massachusetts. Kitty and I had breakfast together; then she left for class. I sat in the lounge of Earlham Hall, pondering the amazing new vitality I felt. I thought the following words. "O God, I wish something dramatic had happened so all this new life won't disappear when I return to my family responsibilities in Cambridge."

Soon I began to be shaken; my body shook as if I had a fever. My jaw dropped and I spoke in tongues or syllables unintelligible to me. I don't know how long I sat thus until I heard footsteps come up the stairs, open the lounge door and ask if I was all right. She must have seen me shaking. When I carefully replied, the shaking stopped. I knew something important was happening to me, but I did not have any idea what. I just sensed it was important to let it continue. So I left the kitchenette and went to Kitty's room. A friend was there, so I sought the common bathroom and entered a cubicle.

I immediately fell on my knees as the only appropriate posture. My arms went upward as I was shaken again. I strongly felt I was in God's presence, and Jesus Christ was off to my left waiting. I was totally overwhelmed with a sense of awe. I could not control the shaking. My jaw mouthed syllables again but this time inaudibly, as if God did not want us to be interrupted.

My upheld arms became weary, my throat became dry, and my knees hurt from kneeling on the tile floor. I sat back on my heels and the shaking stopped. But as soon as I was rested it began again and I rose to my kneeling position. I was not being harmed so it wasn't evil. Maybe God had heard my unspoken wish for something dramatic. If so, that meant God knew all my thoughts!

I was oblivious to my surroundings. I felt like a newborn baby, naked and unprotected in God's Presence. He saw through all my clothes, achievements, actions, age. He knew me completely. It was disconcerting but not dangerous to be so defenseless. I experienced such a complete happiness and awareness of being loved that I asked to become a funnel through which this new bliss could be passed on to others.

My knees and arms cried out for relief, so I rested again. Again the shaking resumed and I was on my knees with raised arms once more. I was enveloped in a total love that had no concern for what I had done or not done in my life. I did not want to ever leave that love.

Kitty returned by noon and found me in the bathroom. I sensed this bliss and mysterious awesome Presence would end if I spoke to her, but I owed Kitty a response to her concern for me.

"Yes, I'm all right, Kitty," I said.

My life has never been the same since. I felt led to enter Harvard Divinity School and become a hospital chaplain at age fifty.

Theodora E. (Dody) Waring *is a lifetime Friend, member of Wellesley Friends Meeting (Massachusetts). She served as a freelance Christian minister and hospital chaplain for 15 years.*

(*What Canst Thou Say?* May 2000 "Traditions That Feed My Soul")

~ ~ ~ ~ ~ ~ ~ ~ ~ ~ ~ ~

A Challenge for Friends

Jean Roberts

George Fox's powerful experiences did not originate with him, nor did they disappear after his death. They continue in people to this day. What is the origin of these experiences and why do they drastically transform lives? The Hindu tradition calls this *"Kundalini* awakening." Early Christians referred to it as the Holy Spirit or the Holy Terror, because of its unpredictable effects. The process that leads to the quickening of this energy has been understood by mystery religions through the ages and has been the goal of yogic practices.... This power was known by many of our great religious leaders, mystics and saints and is the same power that lies in each one of us.

Jean Roberts founded Sky Valley Friends Worship Group (Washington) and helped found WCTS. She continues to educate both Friends and the larger community about the reality of spiritual emergence and mystical experiences. She raises apples and blueberries. Her serene face lights up any gathering.

(Excerpted from "A Challenge for Friends," reprinted from *Friends Bulletin* in *What Canst Thou Say?* in November 2001 "Kundalini Energy")

~~~~~~~~~~~~~

An Interview with Elaine Emily

Elaine Emily is a Quaker healer who has had many mystical experiences since childhood. She spoke with WCTS editor Kathy Tapp about an intense spiritual experience in 1995 which clarified her leading to be a healer, and also about her work with others who are experiencing Kundalini energy.

I was at a workshop led by John Calvi at the Ben Lomond Quaker Center in Northern California. My body began shaking intensely. The shaking and buzzing increased; my whole body buzzed. It felt as if every cell in my body was moving. We did a meeting for healing and during that meeting I shook to the point where I thought my teeth would fall out. Medical people thought I was having a seizure.

Then I had a vision. Buddha appeared in the middle, Jesus to the Buddha's right, and Mohammed on the left. Behind them were row after row—legions— of women healers—all of them throughout time—those from the past and those from the future—races I recognized and races I had not seen before. And the Buddha grew huge, so huge that the whole building was in one chamber of his heart and the legions of women just kept coming and coming and coming. I saw it with my eyes closed and with my eyes open.

It was clear that I was being initiated into that group of healers, and that healing was the work I should do. The buzzing went on for days afterwards. The light was inside me, and some people saw light. I was re-wired from 110 volts to 220 volts. It was also clear to me that it was a Kundalini experience.

It feels like a wonderful gift and a huge responsibility. The healing does not come from me but through me. When I give healing now I go into an altered state and receive guidance, so each healing is a mystical experience. I'm very grateful and honored that this work has come to me. A clearness committee helps me stay grounded in the spiritual work.

As a healer I work with others experiencing Kundalini energy. People first contact me because something out of the ordinary or weird has happened. Their experiences can range from visions to energy surges, to arm or body movements, to spontaneous orgasms while meditating. Often these people feel isolated; others don't understand their experiences. They are either euphoric or terrified. Just having a listening ear helps. I try to help normalize the experience and assure them that it won't always be like this. If they're euphoric, I let them know there might be hard times ahead. If they're terrified, I remind them that the fruits of the Spirit will come.

When they are in this initial stage, I have frequent contact with them. Sometimes even daily; certainly weekly. At this stage, people need to see the process as sacred work, to give the process as much space as possible, to be proactive in allowing space for this. I suggest to them to reactivate or reintroduce their spiritual practice, if the practices are appropriate for their experiences. But meditation may not the best spiritual practice at this stage; it increases the energetic activity. I often suggest journaling, artwork, Tai Chi, swimming, walking. I urge them to pay attention to their physical condition. Many people use words like electricity or energy to describe their experiences, but at the same time, they don't pay attention to the conduit—their body. The stronger the body is, the greater the ability to accommodate large amounts of energy.

After the first rush of energy, people often think they are off the hook. I look at this as break time, time to shift spiritual practices and to reaffirm them. During this phase I encourage them to look at their diet, spiritual practices, relationships, exercise, addictions, and sleep. Unless people are really depressed and sleeping too much, I consider sleep as sacred.

By this time, these people's lives are beginning to change, especially jobs and relationships. If they allow these changes, there's a much clearer sense of their lives being led. At this point, the people who came in euphoric are beginning to hit the more difficult parts. And the people who were terrified are beginning to find some peace. Almost everyone I work with is also working with a therapist. Therapy and spiritual healing work go hand in hand. People's progress is spiral.

I think of Kundalini as the Holy Spirit. But we Christians, although we have good disciplines, don't have the map for experiences like these. If we look at the lives of the saints—they had headaches, episodes of shaking, heat, and were sometimes sickly, ill, isolated. We hear about only the fruits of the spirit. I wonder what the saints did about the hard stuff that I assume came earlier. These bodily manifestations have always been there, but Christians have often ignored them. A number of people have been misdiagnosed as epileptic. While the modern medical model has not been helpful in the past, there are signs of a shift in some places.

By using the map provided by the Kundalini model, these experiences which seem so bizarre and cause people in our society to be described as mentally or physically ill, can be seen as part of a process toward transformation.

When people come in to tell me of their experiences, I say two things: "Congratulations" and "You poor thing." It is a wonderful, sacred roller coaster ride. Since God is in charge, you really can enjoy the thrill. There are people in all of our meetings who are having these experiences. Listening to these people's journeys is sacred work. It's like being in meeting for worship. It's important not to ignore the experiences and also important not to get hooked on and attached to them. To get too attached to such experiences is to prevent the transformation from happening. This whole process is about transformation.

(What Canst Thou Say? November 2001 "Kundalini Energy")

~ ~ ~ ~ ~ ~ ~ ~ ~ ~ ~ ~

In the year 1648, as I was sitting in a Friend's house in Nottinghamshire.... I saw there was a great crack to go throughout the earth, and a great smoke to go as the crack went; and that after the crack there should be a great shaking. This was the earth in people's hearts, which was to be shaken before the Seed of God was raised out of the earth. And it was so; for the Lord's power began to shake them, and great meetings we began to have, and a mighty power and work of God there was amongst people, to the astonishment of both people and priests.[3]   —George Fox (1624–1691)

(What Canst Thou Say? November 2001 "Kundalini Energy")

New Eyes

Connie Lezenby

After my first year of graduate school in architecture, I met with my teachers for a conference and told them I felt as though I had new eyes. It was as if I had never looked at buildings before, and now I could see their beauty and inner structure. I was seeing the old world through new eyes.

There was another time in my life when I woke up to a new dimension of what life has to offer. I had quit my job in order to start my own business and had a lot of time on my hands. I began painting and studying my dreams. I had joined a Quaker meeting as a last gasp attempt to find God. I was reading Marion Woodman and recognizing my need for feminine values in my spirituality. A friend and fellow architect had suggested I look at Shaker architecture and furniture. He also mentioned that a woman had founded the Shakers. I was intrigued and a few days later found myself in a bookstore holding a book on the Shakers. I took it home and before going to sleep I read the story of Ann Lee. I was impressed by the authenticity of her life and her courage. Obviously something profound had occurred to spark the journey she took.

I fell asleep and dreamed I was standing in the center of the Shaker village in Sabbathday Lake in Maine. I was Ann Lee, and people were coming up to me and asking me about the shaking that was happening to me. This wonderful sense of vibrations filled my whole body.

I woke and found that this was happening to me in consciousness also. I was aware of a presence hovering over me and instantly recognized, "Oh. this is God!"

I was filled with fear. Immediately the vibrations were gone, and I felt alone. I lay thinking and wondering, "This is what I have been seeking! This is it!" I relaxed and asked for the experience again. I felt ready. All the sensations returned as if in answer to my request. I have learned again and again that God is not invasive. There is a patient wonderful waiting until there is an invitation to come closer. My request was that invitation.

This is the place where words become difficult. It felt as if there were a huge planet hovering over me and waves of love were overflowing into me. It was as if there were only God and me in the whole world and every ounce of God's devotion was beamed toward me. Undying, unending love, overflowing, radiating love. I thought, "Oh, this is what is meant by 'God is Love.' This is the source of the stories in the Bible. Now I see!"

I began to pray the only prayer I could think of, "Our Father who art in Heaven…" The energy in front of me formed a phallus (there were pictures forming in my imagination) and it felt as if a seed were planted through my navel (George Fox's seed?). There was a crackling sensation speeding through my arms, legs, fingers and toes. I realized it was branches and leaves unfolding. I was a tree. I felt as though I were on fire. Then the feelings and pictures changed, and my body was a rocky cave with a rushing mountain stream flowing through. The visions changed one more time, and I felt my body wriggling and writhing and then realized I was a snake coming out of its skin.

When all had passed I woke my husband and told him my story. He told me my body was really hot. He said lovingly, "You're not a person who would make up something like this." In the morning I was excited, wanting to tell my friends and family, "God does exist! It's true!" A new dimension had entered my life. I saw the world with new eyes.

I told one friend I was afraid both that I would have another experience like the one the night before, and that I would never have that experience again! Two nights later that same vibration awakened me. This time it felt as if a light was planted at the base of my spine which forcefully and energetically burst up through my body and out of the top of my head. It felt as if my head had opened up and the Light was pouring out. In a vision I watched as the Light beamed over rows and rows of books as if in a library. I realized that the books contained all of my thoughts and words since I had been born. The Light (God) was blessing each word. Such joy, bliss, power, and wonder I felt during this experience.

More and more experiences, too numerous to relate, came to me. My friends and family were worried about me when I tried to explain what was happening. This made me worried too. Perhaps I was becoming psychotic. I confided in my friend Lea from my Friends Meeting; she didn't know what this was either. She promised to take my story to Friends General Conference (FGC) and see if anyone there knew about this. At FGC she met Jean Roberts, who gave her a packet of information on Kundalini awakenings to take back to me. It was a real lifesaver. I was able to put my experiences in a context with a language. What was happening was good and natural. My life was simply continuing to unfold and expand.

Part of the information in the packet was about a Kundalini conference coming to Philadelphia. Perfect timing! I went to the conference and in speaking to a small group of women, I related the story of my friend finding me help at FGC. I told them I still remembered the name of the woman who had sent the information: Jean Roberts. They all smiled at me. I looked at one woman and saw her nametag: Jean Roberts. We hugged and laughed. Just when I think there is nothing more for me to learn or experience about life, there is more.

Connie Lezenby *has three children, is an architect, a Spiritual Director and has been clerk of Gwynedd Friends Meeting (Pennsylvania).*

(*What Canst Thou Say?* November 2001 "Kundalini Energy")

A Story for "Slow Leaks"

Patricia McBee

I have been privileged to read *What Canst Thou Say?* since its first issue and have been lifted up by the beauty and courage of the stories people have shared. Those stories strum a deep chord in my being. As I read my breathing slows and deepens, and I find myself in a holy place.

I know myself to be a part of the fellowship of people who have experienced this Presence. But then I am puzzled. How do I know this? I don't have a dramatic story to tell of a moment when awareness of the Presence broke through my consciousness. And then I can feel competitive: Why haven't I had one of those nifty experiences? What do I have to do to get one? And then back to puzzled: If I haven't had one of these experiences, what makes me think I am part of the fellowship?

So I thought I would write my story for others who, like me, are drawn to *What Canst Thou Say?* and the Spiritual Support Network, but have no dramatic stories to tell. I think there are hundreds, maybe thousands, of Friends who have small, frequent experiences of Presence and barely notice them or think of them as part of everyone's experience and not particularly noteworthy.

I was helped a few years ago by reading Philip St. Romain's *Kundalini Energy and Christian Spirituality*.[4] While this book is mainly about the sudden and dramatic rise of Kundalini energy, he also refers to people who experience slow leaks, gradual rising of spiritual energy. I have been pleased since then to think of myself as a slow leak, even though from my childhood that term meant slow to catch on. I like the double meaning; being a slow leak is a humbling corrective for someone who is proud of her quick wit.

Yvonne Kason in *A Farther Shore* refers to different patterns of what she calls spiritually transformative experiences or STEs.[5] She observes that while some may have one notable or profound spiritually transforming experience, others may experience a "slow onset with gradual increase in notable STEs occurring over many years" and others may have "ongoing high STE activity from birth" (pp. 24–25). I find it comforting to think of myself as part of a continuum of persons blessed with a sense of presence, the quiet and gradual as real as the sudden and dramatic.

My story as a mystic begins at age seven or eight, kneeling in my Catholic church just having received my first communion. I experienced a tingling along my spine and a profound sense of specialness. At the time I assumed that it was a normal part of the experience and common among the other 25 children. Nonetheless, I mentioned it to no one. I had many tingles like that, especially in church when something rang true. I never mentioned them either. When I was in ninth grade and kneeling in the choir loft of that same church, I had my first experience of guidance—*Change high schools*. Somehow I explained to my parents my desire to change schools without revealing the impetus. In college, sitting in meeting I was led to change majors—boom! Right there I made a commitment to change. I had never thought about it before, and I have never looked back. I realize as I write this that both of those guided changes led me to opportunities to deepen my spiritual life.

And so it has been for me over more than forty years—periodic tingles and periodic guidance. In recent years they have gained momentum. My first experiences of guidance were separated by several years. Then for a period in the 1980s it was once a year in the quiet of summer vacations. Now, when I keep the pace of my life from becoming too hectic, I can have almost continuous access to guidance which I experience as conversations with a spiritual guide.

I realize from reading and talking to others that Presence comes to us in different ways and at different paces. I have been blessed, so far, with a gentle, gradual opening. I am grateful to *What Canst Thou Say?* for giving us a place to tell our stories, to hear from one another, to ground ourselves in the commonalities of experiencing Presence, and to explore what these experiences require of us in response.

***Patricia McBee** is a member of the editorial team of* What Canst Thou Say? *and a member of Central Philadelphia Friends Meeting (Pennsylvania).*

(*What Canst Thou Say?* December 1996)

~~~~~~~~~~~~~

Giving Birth to the Sun

Marcelle Martin

In 1999, I finally acknowledged I was in a crisis. Although my life seemed wonderful in many ways, I could no longer ignore pain in my heart, chronic fatigue, and other symptoms, physical and non-physical, that told me I was in trouble. The problem seemed to affect every area of my life. I was grateful for some images that helped me get a sense of my condition.

When I prayed about my primary relationship, I saw my partner and me picnicking peacefully in a high, sunny meadow on the side of a mountain, enjoying a good view of the landscape. But I also saw that from this pleasant meadow there was no path to the top of the mountain, our intended destination. To continue our journey, we must walk into dark, rocky woods, and travel over difficult terrain.

I had been having warnings in dreams and during worship about being in a life-and-death crisis. I had an instinctive sense, like that of an animal, of needing to retreat to some dark, quiet, protected place where I could be alone, either to heal wounds, to die, or to give birth—or perhaps all three things. *When I prayed about what changes were necessary in me, an image came of giving birth to the sun in my solar plexus.* Its very name, "solar plexus," suggests the radiating light of the sun, and in some systems of thought, the solar plexus area is connected with personal power.

I was finally ready to consider seriously the Kundalini model. Since 1985 I had been aware that my spiritual development was connected with a whole range of manifestations, including energy moving in my body, ESP and intuition, visions, and strange physical conditions. In the fall of 1995 I had attended the Kundalini Research Network conference held in Philadelphia, where I had met several Quakers from around the country who were also seeking to understand the unusual manifestations that accompanied their spiritual awakening. The conference showcased a wide range of experts, including medical doctors, therapists, yoga teachers, spiritual teachers, and scientific researchers.

The presenter who seemed most spiritually centered, knowledgeable, and able to explain Kundalini comprehensively was a woman named Joan Harrigan. The primary source of the information she shared with us was not her doctoral dissertation on certain yoga practices, but a 500-year oral tradition of Kundalini knowledge. For fifteen years, she had been studying with a Hindu teacher—Swami Chandrasekharanand Saraswati—and was writing about the Kundalini model taught in his spiritual lineage.

Most writing about Kundalini suggests there is only one path the Kundalini energy can travel from the base of the spine to the crown of the head. Joan's model showed six different paths the rising Kundalini can take, four of them intertwined. Only the central paths have connections all the way to the crown. The others are deadends, although they can reach as high as the brain. A rising can have different kinds of manifestations and challenges, according to the particular channel in which the energy rises. In some, the Kundalini can make its slow ascent with few or no peculiar psychic, energetic, or physical symptoms, only a gradual intensification of spiritual focus. People whose risings are peaceful, with subtle effects, may never be aware they are becoming able to channel higher frequencies of divine energy. In others, however, the process can be dramatic, problematic, or seriously challenging to mental or physical health.

Reading about the Hindu spiritual tradition had shed much light on my own spiritual experiences and explained many things I had not found accounted for in Christian teachings. Another Quaker I met at the conference decided to enter a program called Patanjali Kundalini Yoga Care (PKYC) offered by Joan to help those with Kundalini risings. This program involved an assessment of whether the Kundalini had risen yet, where it was, what could be blocking the rising or what weaknesses in the individual might be causing problems. The second stage of the program was to receive recommendations for practices that would support the Kundalini rising. Monthly phone consultations were available, as well as a two-week retreat.

About a month after the conference, I received a message during prayer that seemed to be telling me to enter that program. However, I was certain that I had been called to an increasingly active role in Quakerism, and I also knew that Christian spirituality was becoming more important to me. This didn't seem compatible with seeking help from practitioners of a Hindu path. Also, I believed I couldn't afford the program.

A year later, my friend sent me Joan's book, *Kundalini Vidya*, and told me about her two-week retreat. It seemed that Joan and her teacher had been a great help to her. I was glad, but I didn't want to hear too much about it. I thought I was on another path. Then, in the spring of 1999, when I recognized I was experiencing a mysterious inner crisis, I reread *Kundalini Vidya* and found that it spoke to my condition. It reminded me of many experiences I had had and suggested how they were connected to my spiritual development. I understood that the program supported people in whatever spiritual tradition they were called to.

I continued to be haunted by a persisting sense that I would die if I didn't make some necessary changes. The death of a friend that spring jolted me. She had suffered from great pain that I now believe was connected to a blocked Kundalini rising. Over a six-month period, a slew of doctors and pain clinics had depleted her financial resources, while insisting that her pain had no physical cause; finally she resorted to suicide. For myself, I knew I needed to choose life. The sense of urgency I felt pushed me to act, initiating a process of reclaiming personal power. As I listened more deeply to the call I felt from God, slowly, painfully, I noticed ways my life was not in alignment with this call, and I became more honest with myself and others.

I wrote the three histories required for an assessment from PKYC, a useful process. Their assessment was that the Kundalini had risen in one of the dead-end channels, saying it would be necessary to bring the Kundalini back down to the solar plexus, where it could be diverted into one of the central channels. I was not pleased to read this, but their assessment made sense of many aspects of my experience, including a previously inexplicable and very painful episode ten years earlier, when, apparently, the Kundalini had attempted to make the necessary diversion at the solar plexus. My system had not been strong enough for it. Having the Kundalini in this particular side channel for a long period of time, as in my case, could be very debilitating to the whole energy system, and probably was connected to my chronic fatigue.

This assessment made sense of the image I had received of needing to give birth to the sun at the solar plexus. It also correlated closely with the image of being at a high pleasant place on the side of a mountain, with no path directly to the peak. Praying about how to afford the retreat, I received assurance that God wanted me to do this, and that the means would be provided. God also provided the way for me to have the peaceful, stable lifestyle necessary for the program, when a generous Friend invited me to share her home. For some, celibacy is also a requirement, and I sensed it was necessary for me then. The recommendations I received included a daily program of prayers, meditations, and yoga postures. I was also given herbs, dietary guidelines, and oil to massage into my skin.

For about four months I followed their recommendations, hoping to be well prepared for the two-week retreat. Shortly before I left for Tennessee, while doing my practices, I experienced a great surge of energy in the solar plexus; I was ready for the diversion.

I was given a pleasant room for the retreat. On the wall was a print of the angel of the annunciation, and I felt that I was there awaiting the birth of something with divine origins. Another woman was on retreat at the same time. We did our practices four times a day, ate wonderful Ayurvedic food that we helped Swamiji and Joan cook, took walks outdoors, listened to tapes explaining the Kundalini process, and prayed a lot. I had vivid dreams showing me that there were certain behavior patterns I would have to leave behind forever.

One evening not too long after I arrived in Tennessee, I sat in the armchair in my room feeling rather pregnant, with strong pressure in my lower back and abdomen; I wondered if my "baby" would soon be born. I woke in the middle of the night making a strong spiritual declaration with all my heart and mind and soul and strength; I felt a flash of heat and saw a glowing vision. Later, in the Kundalini literature, I read that this particular vision was one of several traditionally associated with the new stage Kundalini had entered inside me. In the morning I felt peaceful and wonderfully centered in a new way.

Purification of body, mind, emotions, and the energy channels, along with surrender to God, must take place before Kundalini can rise in a healthy way. Once it rises, the purification process intensifies. I had naively hoped that once the diversion to the central channel happened, my fatigue would be completely cured. Instead I learned that I had entered what Joan called a renovation/restoration phase. Kundalini had moved into new quarters and immediately got busy opening closet doors and throwing out psychic debris I had stuffed inside. A brighter light was shining on every darkness in me that separated me from God. It would take time to complete the restoration of my damaged energy system. At the same time, Kundalini would be purifying and strengthening the next area that would be opened up.

Joan told me that it was as if I had a newborn baby; I had to give almost full time attention to this baby in the coming year. I soon learned my plans to take up new commitments right away were not realistic. I also discovered I could no longer tolerate certain kinds of situations and interpersonal dynamics that had seemed acceptable to me in the past.

My experiences on retreat and the guidance I have received from PKYC have pushed me more deeply onto a Christian path. My relationship with God seems to have become more direct and honest; I am more acutely aware both of my failings and of the call to total union with the divine light and love and will.

Today I wonder how my life would have been different if I had sought help from PKYC years earlier, before I reached the point of crisis. How much pain and confusion might I have saved myself and those close to me? I don't know.

Since my retreat in June 2000, I've discovered that the "birth" I experienced at my solar plexus was one small step in a larger, very subtle birthing process that is taking place. Perhaps, in the process of being drawn into the fullness of what it means to be sons and daughters of God, we are called into many rebirths, until ultimately our souls become indistinguishable and inseparable from the Light which is their source.

Marcelle Martin is a member of Chestnut Hill Friends Meeting (Pennsylvania), which has recognized her ministry of spiritual nurture. She teaches and leads retreats and is the author of two Pendle Hill pamphlets: Invitation to a Deeper Communion *and* Holding One Another in the Light.

(*What Canst Thou Say?* November 2001 "Kundalini Energy")

~~~~~~~~~~~~~

I awoke; it was yet dark and no appearance of day or moonshine, and as I opened my eyes I saw a light in my chamber, at the apparent distance of five feet, about nine inches in diameter, of a clear, easy brightness, and near its center most radiant. As I lay still looking upon it without any surprise, words were spoken to my inward ear, which filled my whole inward man. They were not the effect of thought, nor any conclusion in relation to the appearance, but as the language of the Holy One spoken in my mind. The words were, "Certain evidence of divine truth." They were again repeated in exactly the same manner, and then the light disappeared.[6] —John Woolman (1730–1773)

(*What Canst Thou Say?* November 2000 "Visions and Voices")

~ ~ ~ ~ ~ ~ ~ ~ ~ ~ ~ ~ ~

Salt Doll

Kathy Tapp

In my childhood religion classes, I was taught that my body was a temple of the Holy Spirit; I had a soul like a bottle of milk inside me and when I sinned, it got dark like chocolate milk. I was puzzled; I couldn't quite picture where this milk bottle soul was located. Decades later, in midlife, I began feeling great jolts of energy on the edge of sleep and when I meditated. I attended Friends General Conference for the first time that year and took the workshop "Beginning to Pray." The energy jolts had left me feeling fragile. I knew I needed help.

A year later the energy intensified, sending great jolts and spasms of shaking through my body. A friend gave me a book on Kundalini energy. I gave it back, didn't want to hear strange Hindu words, didn't want to think of an energy inside me. Months passed before I was ready to read it, apprehensively. Some sections spoke to my condition; others described things I had never experienced. Was this energy inside me indeed Kundalini? "Is there a western word for Kundalini?" I asked a Quaker friend who knew about this energy.

"I would say that it's the Holy Spirit," she answered softly.

The Holy Spirit. The world had gotten too big. I felt ready to fall off its edges. The energy was an "it," an intrusive force in my life. Something that went through me in waves at night, caused altered states and great fatigue, brought up old trauma and kept me in survival mode. I dreamed of huge ocean waves coming toward me.

At Northern Yearly Meeting's Spiritual Nurture program, we were asked to consider a daily spiritual practice. But the presence of this energy made my days unpredictable with fewer hours to be productive. I had no time for spiritual disciplines; this energy was sabotaging my attempts to get closer to God.

Then one day like a bolt out of the blue, the thought came to me—was it possible it was the other way around? If everything I had read was right, if the people advising me were right, then maybe my spiritual practice was this energy—to relate to it in a different way—to learn how to work with it instead of fight it. If so, then trying to add spiritual things in an attempt to override it and to be master of my day was entirely backward.

I made a retreat at a nearby Benedictine monastery, checked out armloads of books, tried to find answers. On one side of the desk was a book by a Hindu swami: *The Psychology of Enlightenment: Meditations on the Seven Energy Centers.*[7] The book began: "Think of this human body as a musical instrument having seven notes, seven different rates of vibration… so we are here to learn how to create harmonious, melodious music of life. The life-force must be allowed to move freely from note to note, from the base of the spine to the crown of the head."

On the other side of the desk were several books by Christian writers down through the ages. They gave advice on how to live a spiritual life. But when they talked about praying, they spoke of the heart, the mind, the soul—not the body.

Looking at the Eastern book on one side of the desk and the books from my Christian tradition on the other side of the desk, I suddenly understood. Christianity had little practical advice for people experiencing spiritual energetic upheavals. How could I learn to think of my body as a flute—to let the air of spirit blow through, to play the seven notes, the song of my life?

I attended a conference on Kundalini energy. The presenters spoke of the human yearning to merge with the Divine. One presenter likened the Kundalini process to "the ocean reaching out to the little pocket of water," saying we are all manifestations of the One and in the end we merge again. On the conference book table I saw the title, *The Salt Doll Walks into the Ocean.*

The title and the ideas stayed with me, as I continued to struggle with the hugeness of the concepts and this process. Over the next few years I found support from a correspondence program with a Swami from India who greatly helped me to appreciate my own Christian roots, from friends going through similar experiences, from my meeting, my husband, and from the energy itself. It was not going through me in "zaps" anymore, but was bringing moments of peace, light, bliss, and Presence. In the early morning when the energy was the strongest, I began to feel the faint beginnings of a sense of "Thou" instead of "it." My ocean dreams changed; now I was dancing alongside the waves. My whole being struggled to realize that just as this energy was within me, I was within this energy. I sought writers who could help me integrate this knowing. "Our bodies are clay earths suffused with the Divine Imagination," wrote John O'Donohue in *Anam Cara*. And the poet Rilke wrote that we must live the questions and we will grow into the answers.

I continue to try to open to the mystery of Spirit and the awesome idea that the spirit animating the cosmos is the spirit animating our bodies. To shift concepts from milk-bottle-soul to flute-being. My husband pasted a cartoon on my computer: "Do you have change for a paradigm?"

I think now I instinctively chose the right workshop at FGC back in 1989—the year this all began. The transformation that happens in the deepest self—coming to know this Presence as Thou instead of it—*is* beginning to pray. The prayer of the salt doll standing on the shore, listening to the invitation of the ocean.

Kathy Tapp *is on the editorial team of WCTS. Editing WCTS has deepened her awareness of the presence of Spirit in all of us and in all the world.*

(*What Canst Thou Say?* November 2001 "Kundalini Energy")

~~~~~~~~~~~~~

A Dream

Wayne Swanger

In my lifetime I have had less than half a dozen dreams as vivid and meaningful as the one I shall describe to you. I had attended various meetings for worship less than a year when I had this dream. My experience with Quaker worship and literature was very limited at the time. This dream served as an awakening.

In my dream I was a small child of about four or five. There was a large gathering at my grandparents' farmhouse. The relatively small house was filled with adults and children as it often was on various holidays. On this particular occasion the levels of activity and noise were unbearable and I began to cry. No one noticed my discomfort.

I scurried past the old cookstove to the narrow stairway and went upstairs. I sat on the metal-frame bed where I slept when I visited my grandparents for a week or two each summer. The commotion downstairs did not slacken, nor did I feel any relief. I sat alone and sobbed.

It was some time before I noticed the faint sound of the windup clock in my grandparents' adjoining bedroom. At first I heard it intermittently, although it steadily maintained its cadence. I became more attentive and actively sought the sound of the clock. Through my efforts I was able to focus on the sound and hear the clock's continuous soft ticking. In a short while, the sound of the clock became more prominent, although the volume had not increased. The din and commotion from downstairs did not abate, yet I was no longer aware of them. I only heard the sound of the clock. My crying stopped. I was at peace. I smiled.

I awoke, sat up in bed, and said, "That was the voice of God." I felt the same peace and had the same smile on my face that I had in the dream. The metaphor was obvious.

The dream was an epiphany. It validated my interest in silent worship. I understood that because silent worship is unencumbered by well intended sermons, repetitive recitations, and our own joyful noise, it enables us to hear the comforting voice of God. The dream provided a guide for silent worship. The voice of God is ever present. We can hear it and be comforted regardless of our states of mind as we enter worship, if we are attentive and actively seek it.

Daily life occasionally may be difficult because of unbearable levels of activity and commotion, but peace is available by taking the time to seek and listen for the voice of God.

Wayne Swanger attends Oshkosh Friends Meeting and Winnebago Worship Group (Wisconsin). His recent introduction to Friends' literature and worship has made him aware that he had been a Quaker for much of his life and had not realized it.

(*What Canst Thou Say?* November 2002 "Spiritual Metaphors")

~ ~ ~ ~ ~ ~ ~ ~ ~ ~ ~ ~ ~

Transformed by the Spirit

Ray Bentman

When I first started attending Central Philadelphia Meeting of Friends, I found the meeting to be in the midst of a huge and bitter argument. They were discussing whether to take marriages of people of the same sex under the meeting's care.

When I first attended meeting for business, where the arguments were most clearly expressed, I was appalled. The debate had been going on for seven years and seemed to have lost none of its vitriol. It was not at all what I expected from Quakers. And what seemed worse, some people in opposition to such marriages were presenting some of the worst stereotypes about gays and lesbians—generalizations that had been circulating in much of the world for a long time but that were patently false.

To be sure, the opposition came from a small minority. But Friends believe that to be approved any proposal must be in accord with the sense of the meeting. That is, there must be a sense that most members present are in agreement and that no one is strongly opposed to the proposal. There must be the sense that the spirit of the meeting is in accord, as a sign that the will of the Holy Spirit is being expressed. And a minority was, with what seemed to me rather narrow-minded arguments, obstructing an important idea that was supported by most of the members.

After one particularly bitter meeting, I walked home thinking that I would just stop attending Quaker meetings. I had to deal with enough homophobia in the ordinary world without seeking it out. And I was impatient with the Quaker insistence on the sense of the meeting, which I interpreted to mean every idea had to have unanimous approval and that nothing of importance would ever be approved.

At home, I told my partner of my decision to stop attending Quaker meetings. He was not a Friend, but he taught at a Friends school and was a very spiritual person. He disagreed with my resolution. He said Friends at least are dealing with the problem. Homophobia is everywhere but usually half-buried. Quakers had the courage to bring the issue out, to honestly air their thoughts and try to deal with honest disagreement. It was easier, to be sure, to live in a place where such thoughts were genteelly concealed. But unearthing the homophobia, expressing it, and dealing with it openly was the best way to resolve those disagreements, however painful the process might be.

I returned to attending the meeting, still unsettled. The issue was to be taken up once again at meeting for business. I went to that meeting rather in the spirit that I had attended City Council's meeting a number of years before, when they discussed including lesbians and gays in the anti-discrimination bill—interested in the outcome but not intimately involved in it.

But at this month's business meeting the proposal was approved. When the clerk announced his sense that the meeting was in accord with the minute, some started singing a hymn. I didn't know the hymn and still can remember only the first line, which went, "Spirit of the living God, fall afresh on me." To this day I cannot think of that moment without being deeply moved. The years of pain and struggle that had gone into this agreement showed itself with a truly spiritual light. This was no politically correct expression of the latest liberal fad. Rather, it came from deeply within the spirit of everyone present and of the group in genuine unity. I had never before felt so keenly the presence of the Holy Spirit.

After the meeting for business we went into the meeting for worship. The deep sense of commitment and love that glowed in the business meeting (itself a form of worship) was carried over into a meeting devoted exclusively to worship. Person after person, members and attenders, even some people who had just dropped in, rose to express their sense of the Holy Spirit's presence. One man, whom I had never seen before and have not seen since, rose to say that this was for him the most spiritual, the holiest, experience he could recall. It was truly a "gathered meeting" in the sense that all of us were thinking and feeling the same thing; we all felt that we had expressed the truth conveyed by the Holy Spirit, by "that of God in everyone." Certainly God is always present in us. But most of us fully sense God's presence only rarely. And it was almost miraculous that a room full of people could all have that feeling at once.

Shortly after that meeting, I applied for membership. I suppose I have not often experienced such a gathered meeting since then. But the awareness of the presence of the Holy Spirit that was granted to me that day has been with me ever since, strengthening my often faltering belief. A meeting like that, I believe, rare as it is, transforms all those who are so fortunate as to be present.

***Ray Bentman**, a member of Central Philadelphia Friends Meeting, is active on the Drug Concerns Working Group of Philadelphia Yearly Meeting.*

(*What Canst Thou Say?* February 2001
"The Spirit in Meeting for Business")

~~~~~~~~~~~~~

Enraptured by Silence

Alvin Joaquín Figueroa

For many years, while thinking about a religious life through ordination, I had a recurrent dream. *I am wearing a clerical shirt, but right at the moment when I am going to put on my Roman collar, a strange magnetic force prevents me from wearing it. It does not matter how I try, my hands cannot reach my neck, and I remain holding the collar with an excruciating empty sensation.* In my long theological journey, every time I toyed with the idea of a religious life, the dream came back, and the only interpretation I could give to it was that the Divinity did not want my service.

When I was a child I even used to play Mass, instead of war or cowboys. I was raised in San Juan in a Roman Catholic household. The Hispanic family always considered the idea of priesthood a blessing. So after finishing high school, and after a friendly priest convinced me not to join Maryknoll on account of my young age, I decided that once I had finished my degree at the University of Puerto Rico, I would enter the Society of Jesus (Jesuits). Jesuits administered the Catholic Center of the university, and there was a lot of encouragement on the campus for my future life as a priest. The Jesuits gave me a solid foundation in terms of social and political education. These were the early seventies, and they were helping to change things, especially in Latin America. This is how I came to know Liberation Theology and the works of Gustavo Gutiérrez.

I was ready to join these soldiers of Christ... until Eros came into my path. My sexuality awakened at the same time as my desires for social justice, and I fell in love with a Presbyterian man. I shared my life with him for almost seven years.

The Church was ready to liberate the oppressed, but did not respond to my own personal oppression as a gay man in a straight world. That's when I started having my dream: *the white collar in my hands and the invisible force that stopped me from wearing it.* I interpreted the dream in these terms: I am gay, I cannot be a priest. So, I decided to come to the United States to work on a doctoral degree in literature. I stayed away from church matters until I came in contact with the Universal Fellowship of Metropolitan Community Churches (UFMCC).

The same year I got my doctoral degree, I became a member and became very much involved with UFMCC's ministry during the next ten years. UFMCC is a Christian denomination with a special outreach for the gay, lesbian, bisexual and transgender community. At last I had found a place where I could worship and where my sexuality was not an issue. I decided that I wanted to be ordained in this denomination in order to serve God, despite the theological contradictions I was finding in a space where, ironically, fundamentalism was clashing with my leftist Jesuit foundation. My dream came back all over again. *But this time the clerical shirt, for some reason, was distinctively gray. What was wrong with me? Why was God rejecting me?*

Theological conflicts with UFMCC dogmas made me depart from my venture with Protestantism, and I found myself alone with no spiritual home. I was too radical to be in a Protestant denomination of this sort, and my disagreements with Catholic dogma left me no room in that religious house. After thirty years of Catholicism, and ten more of Protestantism, I was not even sure of my Christianity; but my recurrent dream was still present.

I began looking anew for a path that could lead me back to God. But this time I was searching for a spiritual home where sexuality was neither the center of things, nor an issue; and where creeds and formulas could not rule my spiritual life. I ended up visiting a Quaker meeting house. I had read about the Religious Society of Friends and its history, and it was time for me to explore. I was very curious about the nature of an unprogrammed meeting, where there were no planned structures and the worship service was an hour of divine expectation. This non-creedal and expectant religion was the answer, for I never knew the power of silence until that first meeting. I had never before experienced the fulfillment of stillness: how we can feel like monks within the world, and let ourselves be the instruments of God's Spirit.

Suddenly I started to make up definitions: Quakerism was Catholicism without the trimmings; Pentecostalism without the noise; primitive Christianity; rational mysticism... However, since becoming a Friend I have discovered that Quakerism is an individual experience; that not everything in life has a clear answer; and that the Light resides within each one of us. In addition, my new spiritual home has helped me understand many things both Catholic and Protestant that I did not understand before.

Some of us like to call Quakerism alternative Christianity, a Third Way. In truth, what attracts me to this spiritual home is the worship style: the house of silence. If the Spirit moves us, we speak; and there's nothing more comforting than to be in what we call a gathered meeting, where the Spirit manifests itself through many utterances. In this space I find something that was very common to my ancestral history: it is precisely the concept of spiritual immanence rather than transcendence, that saints like Teresa de Avila and John of the Cross articulate very well through their mystic poetry. And it is this type of theological language that I was seeking and have found.

My friends make fun of me. They cannot seem to imagine me in silence or in meditation. To be honest, it is a cultural challenge for a Puerto Rican to be silent for a whole hour. But it is possible, and it works! For me, it is a time for meditation and prayer, and a way to recharge my batteries for the week. But more than anything, it is my source of peace. No space makes me feel the peace I have found in the simplicity of the Quaker meeting. It is a peace I keep on feeling during the rest of the week, simply because the Divine resides in me.

My best friend is now a seminarian for Roman priesthood. About four years ago, he and I sat on one of the walls of my fortress city, overlooking the Atlantic Ocean. It was Christmas time and the blue of the sky was incredibly beautiful: not a single cloud and an overwhelming radiance. We kept on staring at the ocean for about an hour and did not say anything to each other.

This part of the island is known as the "Puerto Rican Trench," and it has the deepest water in the hemisphere. Both of us felt a great sense of communion and spiritual presence while letting ourselves become intoxicated by the sound of the sea and the Caribbean sun. That was when I learned to appreciate silence amid the beauty of my tropics and the gift of friendship. The memory of this moment often helps me center down in Quaker meetings.

By the way, I stopped having that dream! I do not need it any more, because the clerical shirt and the Roman collar were not the answers to my spiritual journey. From the very beginning God was telling me we are all vessels of the Holy Spirit, and there is that of God in everyone.

Alvin Joaquín Figueroa *is a member of Crosswicks Friends Meeting (New Jersey).*

(*What Canst Thou Say?* May 1999 "Dreams")

~~~~~~~~~~~~~~

The Nominating Voice

Elizabeth F. Meyer

I belong to a meeting which has had many wonderful presiding clerks over the years, and those who have never served in that role view the job with awe, feeling they are not spiritually ready to be clerk of the meeting. I was no exception.

About a year and a half before I heard the nominating voice, I was finishing a stint as the clerk of a yearly meeting committee. I had enjoyed my work with that committee, and I was feeling a sense of loss that this term was coming to an end. I felt at loose ends because I did not feel a leading to anything else. Then, in meeting for worship, I was holding this sense of loss in the Light when I received a clear impression that God had other work for me, and I was not supposed to be clerking committees at this time. This impression removed my feeling of loss, and over the next year and a half I resisted attempts by others to get me to serve as clerk of various committees. I did not know what this other work might be, but I was patient and calm when I remembered the impression I had received.

About six months after I received this impression, I began serving on my monthly meeting's nominating committee. I came on the committee when our meeting was struggling to find a new assistant clerk. The assistant clerk serves as a kind of clerk-in-training, and then becomes the presiding clerk in two years. Thus, when the meeting approves a new assistant clerk, it effectively is naming its future presiding clerk. After an extensive search, nominating committee found a person willing to serve as assistant clerk, but some members objected, and the nomination was withdrawn. An acceptable candidate finally was approved, but not before there were many hurt feelings. The whole controversy served to make people even more reluctant to be nominated for assistant clerk.

A year later, I was washing dishes on a sunny winter afternoon. I stood in a pool of light that streamed down from the skylight overhead. I was in a dreamy mood, enjoying the winter sun and letting my mind wander where it would. Thoughts about nominating committee drifted across my mind: how much I had enjoyed service on that committee; how the committee would soon have new members including Barry Morley, one of the spiritual giants of the meeting; how this year we had to find a new assistant clerk.

Then, I heard the voice. It was loud and clear. I did not hear it with my ears, but it was as clear as if spoken by someone in the room. It said, *You know, don't you, Betsy, that when Barry comes on the nominating committee, he will suggest* you *for assistant clerk.*

The voice threw me into a tizzy. I knew the voice had to be right because its authority was so clear, but I felt unprepared, and our meeting's standards were so high. Didn't the nominee almost have to be able to walk on water to be approved? I had thought I might take a turn as clerk ten years down the road, but now seemed too soon. I tried to think of others who could be nominated, and I comforted myself with the thought that we would not begin the assistant clerk search for a number of months.

A few weeks later, the nominating committee met with its new members, including Barry. Someone groaned, "We have to find an assistant clerk this year."

Barry piped up, "That will be no problem this time. I know who it will be." He pointed to me.

It took several months before I felt comfortable accepting the inevitable, and I had to be sure the committee considered other candidates and was comfortable nominating me. As I worked with Barry in the nominating process, I discovered he had a real gift for knowing who should fill which positions. I had to trust Barry was right in my case as well.

Serving my meeting as assistant and then presiding clerk turned out to be a labor of love. I treasured every minute of those four years, especially the many challenges. The constant need to rely on the Spirit for direction and assistance strengthened my faith, and I felt the love and support of the whole meeting. The nomination was exactly what I needed at that point in my spiritual formation.

What was that nominating voice I heard? Was it the voice of God or was it merely intuition putting two and two together in my subconscious? Certainly, I knew certain facts that could add up intuitively: that Barry would come on the committee, and that Barry respected and sought to encourage me. However, Barry was a spiritual mentor to many, and I had no hint he might have seen me in a clerking role. Moreover, the voice spoke with such authority and had such a sense of *other*, that is, not being of myself, that I believe the voice was more than just intuition. I think of it as intuition informed by the Spirit.

Like many Friends, I want to serve God according to the Divine Will, but discernment is a challenge. My experiences of first receiving the impression that there was other work and of later hearing the nominating voice has given me comfort as I continue to seek to discern how God would use me. I feel the promise that God is with me, constantly forming me for future service as I seek to serve in the present. God will lead me step by step, and if I should get lost, God will call me back. I might even hear a voice.

Elizabeth F. "Betsy" Meyer *is a member of Sandy Spring Friends Meeting (Maryland).*

(*What Canst Thou Say?* August 2004 "Knowings")

~~~~~~~~~~~~

It is an overwhelming experience to fall into the hands of the living God, to be invaded to the depths of one's being by his presence, to be, without warning, wholly uprooted from all earth-born securities and assurances, and to be blown by a tempest of unbelievable power which leaves one's old proud self utterly, utterly defenseless, until one cries, "All Thy waves and Thy billows are gone over me!"(Ps 42:7). Then is the soul swept into a Loving Center of ineffable sweetness, where calm and unspeakable peace and ravishing joy steal over one. And one knows now why Pascal wrote, in the center of his greatest moment, the single word, "Fire." [8]   —Thomas Kelly (1893–1941)

(*What Canst Thou Say?* May 1999 "Kundalini Energy")

~~~~~~~~~~~~

A Numinous Presence

Alison Lohans

It was early December, 1984, the eve of my fifteenth wedding anniversary. For thirteen of those years, my husband Michael and I had been enduring both the trials, and the fervent, breath-holding hopes, of living with his testicular cancer.

Clinically, he had two types of cancer. Mercifully, perhaps, it was the less malignant strain which kept recurring, and which bought us thirteen and a half unexpected years following that first horrific exploratory surgery. During those years the cancer traveled its erratic route through his body: it claimed a kidney and two or three ribs; it lodged itself in his spine three times, made repeated visits to his lungs, and wreaked havoc when it reached his brain. Yet over those years of surgery, radiation and chemotherapy, my husband consistently kept winning; the cancer always went into remission. And so he completed a Ph.D. and went on to a much-longed-for university teaching position. Within these bouts of relative wellness our lives had a semblance of normalcy, regularly punctuated by the stresses of major illness. Michael took good physical and spiritual care of himself. We knew that many people were praying for him/us.

However, there came that inevitable downward spiral. The human body and spirit can only endure so much. Likewise, a terrible toll had been exacted on our relationship. A third close call with paralysis in 1983 was remedied by reconstructive spinal surgery. Brain surgery in 1984 severed a nerve and left him unable to read. Four months later, a mechanical breakdown in his spine once again sent him to the hospital. This time surgery didn't work. The incision, made in irradiated skin, did not heal. Confined to a wheelchair, my husband lost the will to live. By December, he had pneumonia so severe that he was hallucinating and unable to recognize anyone. Both of our mothers and his brother came from California and Oregon into a frigid Canadian prairie winter to be with us. We suspected it might be the end.

The eve of our anniversary found him on oxygen and talking to "people in the air." It found me terrified, emotionally raw with nerves stretched taut, and with an academic deadline that could not possibly be met. With this came an overwhelming feeling of having been betrayed, as I confronted the reality that my husband might very likely die soon. He had not recognized me for the past few days. And recent years had been so acutely stressful that he, in his misery, had become emotionally abusive and I, the sole caretaker outside the hospital, had become the victim. It was a scenario of anger and resentment, instead of one in which loving goodbyes could be said.

Daytime temperatures hovered at -20 degrees F, a potentially killing cold. Fern-like frost patterns sketched their beauty across windowpanes. The sun shone with a stark, revealing purity on the vast prairie whiteness, and ice crystals glittered in the air. In my husband's hospital room, the hissing suction drew great globs of mucus from his lungs while oxygen flowed in, and rust-brown urine filled the bag. "His kidneys have failed," the nurse told me. "He may not last the night." I told her he had only one kidney.

We kept vigil in his room: myself, his mother, and his brother. My own mother was caring for our child in our home. One of Michael's friends (and department head) came for a visit and saw the gravity of the situation. Ernie, a devout Mennonite, offered to come back later to read from the Bible, and to pray for a gentle passing. We all thought this would be a very good thing. And so Ernie left, to return at midnight with a thermos of coffee, homemade bran muffins, and a Bible. I don't remember the verses he read; they weren't familiar to me. And then Ernie prayed, letting Michael know that if it was time, he should feel free to go, with our love and blessings.

A numinous Presence hovered in the room. There was a sense of precarious balance. And then came a shift, followed by a feeling of peace. Needing to go to work later that same morning, Ernie went home. I lay in the hospital bed with my husband, exhausted and knowing this might be the end—but also feeling that if and when it happened, things would be all right. A few hours later, Michael opened his eyes. He was lucid and wanted milk. Due to his congestion, we gave him tea instead. Later, in his feeble hand, he scrawled some thoughts he'd been having about his medications onto a paper towel. It was our fifteenth wedding anniversary.

Michael died the following July. He waited for my birthday and then, within two weeks, let go. During those precious seven months, we caught up on all the important things that had gone unsaid. Together, we learned some wheelchair basics which allowed me to take him for drives in the car, and for overnight home visits. Love returned to our time together.

Since then paths have diverged, and I no longer see Michael's relatives or Ernie. However, in occasional phone calls and correspondence, that visitation is mentioned every now and then. We all felt it: the Light of that numinous Presence, that shift, that mystery. All these years later, I am still humbled by that grace and power, and by the hugeness of that loving, healing gift.

Alison Lohans grew up in Fresno Friends Meeting (California) and for many years has been a member of Prairie Friends Meeting (Regina, Saskatchewan).

(*What Canst Thou Say?* November 2003 "Spiritual Healing")

God in Nature

The world of life, of spontaneity, the world of dawn and sunset and star-light, the world of soil and sunshine, of meadow and woodland, of hickory and oak and maple and hemlock and pineland forests, of wildlife dwelling around us, of the river and its well-being—all of this some of us are discovering for the first time as the integral community in which we live. Here we experience the reality and the values that evoke in us our deepest moments of reflection, our revelatory experience of the ultimate mystery of things.[9]

—Thomas Berry, 1988

(*What Canst Thou Say?* February 1999 "Nature")

We can be restored and nourished by experiencing God's creation and our oneness with it. We feel the universe as one organic whole, held together by the radiating power of love flowing through everything. In "Oneness with Nature" Mary Waddington single-handedly aids a beached porpoise, communicating without words her intent to help, maybe even her plan of action. Dorothy Mack communes with a mountain sheep on its own turf, and the mountain sheep teaches her how to be ("To Walk in This World, Yet Not of It").

Several of our writers draw life lessons from their encounters with Nature. When Hazel Jonjak's Bronco mortally wounds a deer in "A Deer Shall Lead Thee," Hazel finds neither fear nor anger in the dying deer; the deer gives her life to Hazel with an amazing sense of blessing. Teenager William R. Stimson runs headlong into a forest clearing—and finds himself completely surrounded by a mat of deadly pit vipers ("Snakes, Orchids, and Novels"). He retraces his steps, learning that a Greater Power kept him from stepping on a single snake. In "Seedlings" Elspeth Colwell helps plant trees, and comes to see her prayers for others as similarly nurturing seedlings. Amy Perry in "This Desert Land" makes a retreat at a monastery in the desert and finds God in the evening stillness.

An expanded awareness of all God's creation makes a lasting impression in Christine O'Brien's earliest memories of growing up on a farm ("Art and the Light"). In "Coming off the Mountain" Brad Sheeks enters a supermarket immediately after a three-day vision quest, and finds himself so spiritually awakened even a detergent box has a deeper message. What has he missed in his blindness? Ken Tapp takes his camera into his garden ("Focusing on the Experience") because the world is a sacred place and a sacred process. May these writers help make us aware it all comes together in love—God's love for us and all creation, and our love for God and all the natural world.

~~~~~~~~~~~~~

Art and the Light

Christine O'Brien

My earliest memories are of the ecstatic feeling of oneness with the natural world filled with God's quiet breathing. Swinging high in my swing beneath the black walnut tree, I felt myself a part of the house, the barnyard, the road, the tiny stream, the very air itself. Sitting at my grandmother's kitchen table, we read a Bible verse every day. Her favorite was, *This is the day the Lord has made: let us exult and rejoice in it.*[10] The things that unfolded at her kitchen table became my sacraments: the vegetables gathered in the garden and put up into red-, green-, and yellow-filled Mason jars; the noodles rolled out, cut, and left to dry; the honey with its drowsy bees brought into the back porch, then glowing in its comb in rows of jars.

This—the colors, the sunlight, the unfolding, the attention, the intention, the sacred process of the beauty of the things of my everyday life—is how I came to want to make art. Today my home is filled with art of all kinds. There are paintings by me, my grandfather, my daughter, my friends. I look at them every day and never grow blind to them. They glow like those Mason jars on the shelves of Grandma's pantry, harvested in some other summer, illuminating this moment, food for the future.

Eating—each meal, the beauty of the leek or lettuce, the knife carefully used, the cast iron skillet tended with love, every bite tasted and savored— is a sacrament to me. Something dies so I can live. Art is a sacrament too. Something is created that calls us to experience the clouds, the flowers, the teacup.

Light is at the heart of all this. In the real world, it allows us to see the colors and forms; it causes the food to grow; it allows us to see the beautiful. In the world of spirit, it illuminates our path and where we are on it, to grow toward the beautiful. I know the darkness of the injustice and violence that people can create, and I know art can reveal these truths, but for me, the gratitude I feel for the beautiful world is what I hold up in my paintings.

Through these sacraments born of light, I bow to the natural world's beauty and the possibility of beauty in each beloved child of God.

Christine O'Brien has retired from clerking the St. Petersburg Friends Meeting (Florida) for nearly 24 years. She has been an activist since she was a teenager.

(*What Canst Thou Say?* May 2002 "Arts and the Spirit")

~~~~~~~~~~~~~~

Oneness with Nature

Mary Waddington

I began having special communications with creatures when I was in my late twenties. My first experience took place in the garden while I was picking raspberries. A motionless grasshopper was perched on a cane very near my face but outside of my focus. When I noticed him our eyes made a prolonged, unwavering contact. A heightened awareness took place, and somehow we went beyond ourselves and into each other. I finally broke the spell because of an urgency to share this phenomenon. I rushed inside and told my husband, who then ridiculed me and suggested that I had lost my senses. First I felt hurt by his response and then I doubted the validity of the experience. Years passed before I again spoke of it.

A second happening, more complex and profound than the first, came much later and assured me that I was sane. One summer day I followed an urge to turn down a long dirt road that led through marshes, assuming I was drawn to do so for a bird sighting. The road eventually dead-ended at an uninhabited, isolated stretch of beach on the Delaware Bay, not far from my home. My eyes quickly spotted a beached dolphin thrashing in the edge of an ebbing tide. Snatching off my shoes as I ran to him, I squatted at his head in the shallow waters of a recess in the beach where he lay. His skin was red and abraded from struggling against the sand. Instinctively I put my hands on his body and crooned soft words of comfort, and immediately he ceased his struggling. Looking into his eyes, which seemed amazingly human, I watched his panic quickly dissipate.

We then communicated through our eyes, with perfect understanding, a rescue plan seemingly jointly conceived, to be executed in partnership. Each time an exceptionally large wave hit shore and surrounded us with water, we would together lift up while I pushed seaward. In this manner, patiently utilizing buoyancy, we inched our way toward his freedom. The bonding that took place between us during this process created an intimacy that was akin to falling in love.

When the dolphin could finally float, he began moving parallel to the shore. I was worried that something was wrong with his radar and he might beach again, so I ran with him along the shoreline, mentally encouraging him to turn toward deeper water. And so he did this. Soon he was arching, cavorting, reveling in his freedom dance. I stood in the edge of the water watching this leave-taking, seeing his glistening back break the surface of the water again and again, until these distant flashes looked like a hand waving good-bye. It was only then that I realized my face was wet with tears.

Often since that summer day the image and essence of this brave, free dolphin will slip back into my mind and heart, and I will have the strong sense at those moments that he is also thinking of me.

A third experience I want to share took place five years ago while I was at an Omega conference in the Caribbean. I was snorkeling in shallow water and came upon a small cluster of golden fish faces peering out from beneath a rock. I drew my extended arms in with a "come here" gesture and the fish were pulled toward me, I supposed, by the current this movement created. We eyeballed each other for a while in studied curiosity and I then pushed my hands outward, causing them to back into their original position under the rock. We played this game of advance and retreat several times with obvious enjoyment until gradually the fish began taking the lead and I was obliged to follow.

I then came upon a large school of sleek silvery fish swimming in tight formation. Now, feeling like a fish myself, I drifted into their center and we swam together. I began to notice that as my arms stroked through the water, the school of fish took on each new configuration my body made. We remained a tight group with always the same tiny distance between each one of us, the fluidity of our boundaries changing shape to replicate the form of my swimming body. We were one pulsating unit with no differentiation between us. We were moving as One in the greater sea of Oneness.

These mystical experiences, combined with others that I've had, have changed my life. I cannot now look into a pair of eyes without seeing the Divine, or step into another's energy field without merging on some level with that person or creature. How blessed I feel to know the sacredness of the holy Oneness.

Mary Waddington *is a member of Salem Meeting (New Jersey).*
(What Canst Thou Say? February 1999 "Nature")

~~~~~~~~~~~~~~

My sunrise meditation means more to me now than ever. At dawn it is eas-ier to feel the universe is one organic whole, held together by that Radiating Power of Love which flows through everything, including thee and me.[11]
— Rachel Davis DuBois (1892–1993)
(What Canst Thou Say? February 1999 "Nature")

~~~~~~~~~~~~~~

A Deer Shall Lead Thee

Hazel Jonjak

In the months leading to the US invasion of Iraq in March of 2003, I vigiled with others in our small town. I placed throw rugs ("Persian" and American) on the icy parking lot, hung words of hope written on dishtowels and pillow cases on an old-fashioned drying rack, and held a blue and green earth flag my 85-year-old mother had sewed. My four-year-old grandson often stood with me, and when airplanes flew overhead my womb contracted with the fear of what planes over Baghdad would mean to Iraqi families. A double-vision of this reality (dark-windowed Suburbans and pickups whizzing by the Kwik-Stop across the street from our peace witness) and Near East reality (grandparents, mothers and fathers, children poised in fear of U.S. power) forced me to express my heartache with the simplest and most utilitarian household materials: cloth, wood, and diaper pins.

When the attack on Iraq was announced we vigilers gathered the next evening at our local Tree of Peace, an *Arbor vitae*, planted in ceremony by Jake Swamp of the Mohawk nation some twenty years ago. The flames from our candles and the songs of perseverance we sang couldn't comfort me or stop my crying.

I retreated to my lair, a one-room house in the woods. Near morning, from my dream world *I glimpsed a mother and child antelope pass by the window at the southeast corner of my home. They were a subdued reddish-brown, with the little one behind its mother, quietly continuing their journey toward a logging path to the west.*

With their brief presence in my world I was soothed. These exotic pronged antelope, kindred to our white-tailed deer (*waawaashkeshiwag*) gracefully entered our north woods, radiating quiet centeredness. Then, at a thrift shop, I happened upon a four-inch pronged antelope created of paper and glue. It was red-orange, with touches of golden iridescence. I placed this kneeling antelope at the top of my bookcase, kitty-corner to my bed, to remind me of the peace and acceptance of the dream-visitors.

At about the time of the planting of the Tree of Peace twenty years ago, I had been scared in an encounter with a flesh and blood deer. My daughter and I had been driving to my brother's home at dusk. With no warning, a winter-starved doe ran into the side of our maroon Bronco. She was terribly hurt, unable to move, with two of her legs broken. As I placed my hand on her head and looked into her eyes, I was astounded that this deer which I had fatally injured communicated no fear or anger towards me. (Perhaps I had expected her to try to bite or get away from me, but it was more like an intimate connecting.) The deer had to be put down and there was no way I could do it.

A friend drove by, and stopped to put the deer out of its misery. We placed the body in the back of the Bronco, and I drove on tremulously. My brother helped me gut the deer, and we found only twigs and bits of popple bark in her stomach. I took the carcass home and hung it outside to cool—but couldn't return to normal myself. In an awful enactment of Ojibwe sharing of my "first kill," I gave meat to friends and family, but could not bear to partake of the deer myself.

A couple of days later an Ojibwe elder came to visit. When I told him of the death of the deer, Bill told me I needed to put *asemaa* (tobacco) down to honor the spirit of the deer. After he left, I placed tobacco on the hide of the deer. Immediately I was comforted. The giving of tobacco placed the incident into the realm of the sacred—out of the grotesque. And with Bill's help, later that spring I scraped and stretched the hide, noting how visceral and pungent life, death, and transforming-of-hide can be. (Bill had me soak the hide for three days so that the hair would slip off more easily!)

In my experience the antelope dream after the attack on Iraq and my killing of the deer (or the deer's offering her life to me) are connected. The antelope and deer brought an image or energy to smooth out my habitual agitated righteousness. The bombing of Iraq struck me especially hard, knowing that our Indo-European roots are shared with the ancient civilizations of the Near East, and that the U.S. was re-enacting barbaric ignorance and oil-lust against relatives. With my own killing-encounter of the most gentle of a gentle species, I, too, have shared the aggressor position, and was healed only with the grace of my counterpart, the deer.

With one last deer-car encounter, and death, I have now given up my car and driving. On November 14, my grandson and I were driving a car loaded with squash from my mother's garden. When we passed the tiny town of Birchwood, Wisconsin, a young forked buck came from the woods so quickly we didn't even see him until he was sliding up our hood to be tossed fifteen feet into the air. The buck hit a pickup coming from the opposite direction, and was dead when he hit the ground. I placed tobacco on his body and gave up my largest complicity in oil-consumption. Neither my grandson nor I were hurt, and now I walk the five miles to the college where I work sometimes, unless I catch a ride. (I'm not completely pure!) The little antelope remains on my bookshelf, and the deer I meet on my travels are no longer in danger from me. And when the U.S. goes resource-grabbing, I don't feel personally implicated through lifestyle guilt.

Indinawemaganadag (all my relations).

Hazel Jonjak appreciates the Inner Light and receptive attitude and peace witness of Quaker practice. She also values going to sweat lodges and living in the woods for insights and guidance.

(*What Canst Thou Say?* May 2004 "Guidance")

~ ~ ~ ~ ~ ~ ~ ~ ~ ~ ~ ~

Mystics report that every bit of the world radiates from one center—every cricket, every grain of dust, every dream, every image, everything under the sun or beyond the sun, all art and myth and wildness. If they are right, then we have no more important task than to seek that center.[12]

—Scott Russell Sanders, 1985

(*What Canst Thou Say?* May 2001 "Solitude")

~ ~ ~ ~ ~ ~ ~ ~ ~ ~ ~ ~

Knowing We Are Home

Carol Cober

When we finally see
that the door is open
there is not a single syllable we can utter
just an awe so staggering
we drop to our knees and
lie belly against the mud, toes and fingers
stretched as if to heaven.

Breathing in the musty scent of leaves
transforming death into new life
throats raw from our cries
we surrender
to that which we have always known
and can never explain.

In that moment when
everything has been given
nothing taken
Light falls on our suffering and joy
equally.
All is precious.

We enter our bodies as holy
and fall down
laughing
holding each other as miraculous
feeling embraced by the earth
amazed life has chosen us
once again.

Carol Cober is a member of Sandy Spring Friends Meeting (Maryland).
(*What Canst Thou Say?* February 1999 "Nature")

~ ~ ~ ~ ~ ~ ~ ~ ~ ~ ~ ~ ~

This Desert Land

Amy Perry

Having plenty of time stretching out ahead of me makes me feel very free and relaxed. I have time to do whatever I want at Our Lady of Solitude in the Arizona desert. I can leaf through the hermitage guidebook with its quotations on silence and solitude, read the book Sister Therese has lent me (which on two occasions has turned out to be just the book I needed), draw with my markers, write in my spiral notebook journal, do a little bit of yoga (being sure to stay far enough away from the icon of Christ on the lace-covered table in the icon corner), do centering prayer, carefully draw the vertical blinds back so I can see out the sliding glass doors, go for a long walk, fix oatmeal or salad or a peanut butter sandwich, wash my dishes, push the hand-powered sweeper over the carpet, or walk down the road to the circular white chapel. There I can go inside to read or pray, or I can sit outside on the bench overlooking the eastern valleys.

Sure, I sometimes miss my loved ones, and I think occasionally of my colleagues at work. But I love just sitting and looking, or standing and looking, or walking and looking. I love to stare outside from my hermitage. During the day sometimes I choose a shadow to keep tabs on and watch its tip retreat across the sand from one rock to another. I like to gaze at the bumpy earth, the occasionally glinting gravel paths, the un-identifiable scrubby plants, the waving of the gray ocotillo limbs, the tan mesas green-polka-dotted with what I know are saguaros, the blackish foothills, the purple mountains behind them, and the tiny red taillights of the cars and trucks as they wind up the bare thin stripe of I-17, disappear behind the hills, and reappear higher up.

As I'm out walking, sometimes a movement catches my eye and alerts me to a bright-eyed jackrabbit who gracefully leaps, then stops, then leaps again; or to a Gambrel quail, her curly crest held high and her little ones toddling along after her. Or I hear the *kree* of a hawk over the hum of the cars. Or I just find a flat rock to sit down on and watch the ants march by.

Sometimes when I'm inside my hermitage reading, the chattering of sparrows makes me look up. Three or four of them will be flitting around the porch railings and talking to each other. I feel sort of as if they are honoring me with a visit. I like the constantly recurring *whirr-rrrrrrrr-aiaiaiaaannnhhhhh*'s of the frogs. From somewhere out beyond my porch a soft buzz emanates, sharpens, and fades away. From somewhere else out beyond my porch another soft buzz emanates, sharpens, and fades away. From somewhere else ... floating, hovering, the stark calls cover the land, just as the desert covers the earth, just as ... God ... inhabits it all.

In the evenings, I like to glance across the way at Sister Therese in her red-checked dress and white tennis shoes as she paces her porch and prays. Then I hike up the paved road to the main mesa to make my nightly circuit as I watch the sun drop behind the next-highest notch in the western mountain ridge. I feel the air cool on my arms. I like to notice when the tan shades of the ground ahead of me take on a subtle pinkish purple tint, then shift to gray, then disappear in the darkness.

I watch the colors darken in the sky above The Sleeping Woman mesas to the southeast, above the low sloping hills to the south, above the long overlapping ridges to the southwest and west, above the Faraway Mountains to the northwest, and above the Sliced Mesa and the Rampart Mesa to the north, above the Thumb outcropping in the northeast, above the Three Purple Friends mountains to the east. I tilt my head back and look for the Swan, then turn my head left and hope it's dark enough for the Big Dipper to be visible. Sometimes, to my delight, I see a shooting star.

When I've drunk in enough, I make my way down the dark road to where I know it will fork. I head right, toward where I know my hermitage is. Getting ready for bed, I have all the lights turned off except for the small desk lamp, and I leave the blinds open so I can see the taillights snaking along and see the lit windows of Black Canyon City scattered below me. After I turn off the desk lamp, often I step out on the northern porch to take a last look at the stars, my nightgown billowing in the wind.

I feel closest to God when I'm in the vastness of the desert. Having time in solitude there gives me time to experience God. I think Hosea 2:16 has it right: *I will lead her into the Desert and speak to her heart.*

Amy Perry *makes silent retreats at Our Lady of Solitude Contemplative House of Prayer in Black Canyon City, Arizona. She is a member of First Friends Meeting (Indianapolis).*

(*What Canst Thou Say?* May 2001 "Solitude")

~~~~~~~~~~~~~

Seedlings

Elspeth M. Colwell

To the north lies a wondrous wild forty. To the south lies a long, heavily wooded pathway leading down to three earth-sheltered houses where we live. It takes ten to fifteen minutes to hike from home to the high plateau. Until now it has been nine acres of thick brome grass hedged increasingly with blackberry bushes, sumac and aspen.

Twice a year our taxes have been reduced by an agreement to allow the Department of Natural Resources (DNR) some jurisdiction over our forested land. This spring our community was approached to allow the nine acres to be planted with nursery seedlings. The DNR would supply the seedlings, we would plant them, and they would inspect. Once bills were paid, a small hourly wage and a schedule of work hours were agreed upon.

The clearing of the nine acres began. Friends spelled each other to create long rows about three feet apart through the grass. I picked up seedlings and the thirty-pound pointed spades at the forestry office. Soon, anyone with a free hour or two came to help carry up the moist red oak, white cedar, and white spruce seedlings to be tucked into the soil.

The routine was: dig, plant, (close-up, so no airholes), move on three steps, continue. Some workers had short strides, others took four long strides. Some rows became ram-rod straight; others followed the curve of the land. Some participants created long rows of one variety, others preferred mixing cedar, spruce, oak, cedar, spruce, oak. After about a month, all three thousand seedlings were planted.

As we rested from our labors, the spring rains came and the blessed sun shone. In between our precious seedlings, dormant wildflowers, many small bushes, and other vegetation sprang up.

Eventually, discovery time arrived. This phase required a glove or two, clippers, a bag of plastic strips, a bottle of drinking water, and snacks. Ready! Three steps forward. Stop. Exultation! Yes, a visible seedling! Stoop. Trim away the weeds, tie on a marker. "May the Great Spirit give you what you need." Move on. Nothing. "Am I standing on you? Little one, show me. Where are you?" Search. Move on.

The joy of discovery time was the eager anticipation of the find. The oaks seemed glad to be recognized; they stood out stiffly, even when their stems were bent. The cedars that thrived had a good color, spread out and reached up. It is said that they have a sweet taste and many critters like to eat them. Some of the spruce rose up straight and jaunty; others were tucked down and barely made a showing. They all received special attention.

The sight of a cluster of sumac crowding one area caused deep dismay. Trees that were dormant in April leafed into full foliage across many paths, blocking any hope of tracing seedlings. Despite these frustrations, I was charmed to be able to bend over those seedlings I found. I watered them with the perspiration from my face, as I trimmed, tied, and gloated over their achievement.

These seedlings help establish for me that God is all there is. Recently I read three quotations that seem to fit the metaphor of prayer and seedlings: *Work as if you don't need the money.* Plant nine acres, write down your hours (the DNR reward might be a long time in coming!) Live twenty years to see development. *Dance as if no one is looking.* We sowed the seed, tramped it in, some seeds among the rocks, others among the thistles and some in the good soil. Birds ate some, some dried up, some were choked by weeds. *Love as if you've never been hurt.* Our meeting has a Prayer List: my daughter and I daily support those whose names are on it. I have come to believe the sons and daughters of God appearing on the prayer list are my seedlings.

For those whose situation is critical: with chronic illness, in surgery, with fractures, the mentally ill, my response might be, "I see you healthy, whole and free." For those with addictions, those who are incarcerated, the homeless, my response might be, "I affirm that the power of God is working within you to bring about the best possible outcome." For those deep in despair, who face diminishments, those in need of guidance and support, I respond, "My sister, my brother, as you open your heart to receive, peace and joy I offer you now."

I have been given a rich gift and when I meet someone from the Prayer List, the seedling glow must surely come into my eyes. Unbeknownst to them, I will be delighted to meet them and converse with them. Settling in meditation, my seedling F/friends appear rooted and grounded, nourished in the Light.

Elspeth Colwell is a member of a small worship group in Wisconsin that meets on a rocky outcropping (beyond the seedlings) 52 weeks of the year. They dress appropriately to the weather and spend some of the hour in silent walking.

(*What Canst Thou Say?* November 2002 "Spiritual Metaphors")

~~~~~~~~~~~~~

Coming off the Mountain

Brad Sheeks

One hundred radios in the room with the volume turned way up. That's the way it sounded as I walked into the grocery store in a small town just south of Yosemite Park.

Along with five others I had just come down from a mountain after a seven-day intensive vision quest experience. I had been away from the noises of everyday life—cars honking, radios blaring, television, phones ringing. I had been in the company of shale stone cliffs, scattered pinion pine trees and blue sage brush. Three of the seven days were spent in solitary fasting silence, practicing spiritual disciplines, seeking a vision of how to live in greater attunement with life itself. At night as I viewed the landscape with its crystal clear air, bathed in the white light of the full moon, I had the feeling of being held in a deeply peaceful, sacred silence.

In the grocery store, by contrast, the check-out machines called out to me from each of the half dozen counters. Clattering, they demanded my full attention. I recoiled from, but was also drawn by, the noise. I stopped and looked at every customer in the store. There was something about each one, an expression, a movement, perhaps something overheard, that gave me the urge to start a conversation, as if we knew one another. I felt a connection to each person. Every item on the grocery shelf called out, "Look at me!" I would stop and look, fascinated by the color and design of a box of laundry soap.

As I reflect on that experience, from the perspective of how to be open to the Spirit and also grounded in mother earth, I realize that I habitually screen out, not only the usual noise and distractions of our everyday lives, but also a sense of being deeply connected to my life. The laundry soap box, as exciting as it may be, sits quietly on the shelf unless I have "laundry soap" on my shopping list. I don't notice the other people in the store as I go down the aisle.

I not only screen out laundry soap, but I also screen out the Spirit when I don't put it on my list for the day. The Spirit is hiding in plain sight, beneath the surface of things I encounter during the day. The Spirit is hiding behind the clerk who asks, "Can I help you?" The Spirit is hiding behind the near miss I just had in traffic, the palms of my hands sweaty as I grip the steering wheel. The Spirit is hiding behind whoever gets the prize for Most Obnoxious Person of the Day.

Coming off the mountain, it was easy to see the Spirit hiding behind the ordinary. Once off the mountain the task is to move slowly enough, enabling that which is hidden to become visible.

Brad Sheeks *is a member of Central Philadelphia Meeting. He works as a hospice nurse and is married to WCTS editor Patricia McBee.*

(What Canst Thou Say? February 2004 "Open and Tender")

~ ~ ~ ~ ~ ~ ~ ~ ~ ~ ~ ~

Quaker Sunset

Keith Maddock

1

These vermillion clouds
colour a horizon green and blue
with gray fading into golden hues,
the earth's breath sighs
of days when people walked
and talked and even loved
upon its broad terrain
of heart-felt happiness and pain.

The sunlight settles into night—
westward springs the harvest moon,
like a soul awakening
in search of an eternal resting place,
borne on an ocean of darkness,
in search of an ocean of light.

2

An inner light
sets or dawn-springs in the heart
when earth and sky
unite in the sublimity
of nature's hard-won harmony
of storm and stillness,
darkness and light.

The sunset in your hair,
the moonlight shining in your eyes
these eternal colours
of the moment radiate
from the light within
to the promise of eternity.

Keith Maddock *is a member of the Toronto (Ontario) Meeting, and a frequent contributor to* The Canadian Friend, Friends Journal, *and* Quaker Life.
(*What Canst Thou Say?* August 2003 "Celebration and Thanksgiving")

To Walk in this World, Yet Not of It

Dorothy Mack

It's always been hard for me to follow in George Fox's footsteps, walking cheerfully through the world, being in it, yet not of it. Not until I went into the wilderness, specifically the Targhee Teton Wilderness, on the hidden Idaho side of the park, did I discover something like George Fox's cheerful way. I love hiking high alpine meadow lush in August with purple monkshood and lupine, red paintbrush, and the dense low mat of mosses and berries. I love high granite peaks, stars, and silence.

My destination that day was Little's Peak, 10,700 feet high. Directly across the valley, rising into the clouds, were the Tetons, seemingly close enough to reach out and touch; the jagged, massive triangular Grand Teton, then the lesser Tetons in a line fading to the south.

On my map Little's Peak was an easy climb, rising steep and steady without cliff faces, ledges or chimneys. It wasn't so much a mountain as a giant scree pile of rocks and boulders, granite chunks cracked and dumped as the glaciers receded.

As I climbed I discovered the steep rock pile was only one side of Little's Peak. The east side was gone—gouged out, sliced off by the same glaciers that deposited this scree. I crouched at the edge. It dropped straight down 2000 feet or so, straight down into glacial ice fields and jeweled lakes, glowing milky blue green. From the Grand Teton, this rock pile must have looked like Yosemite's Half Dome.

There was no trail, only scree-hopping to the top. The easiest route followed the ridge or backbone four feet from the drop-off—loose shifting rubble four feet from disaster. Spectacular, but it made me cautious. I floundered, slipping and scraping myself on the scree. Rocks I loosened ricocheted and clattered down the mountain.

The weather wasn't so great. In August the Tetons are usually clear in the morning, clouding up for rain in the afternoon. This day, though, it was cloudy, windy and cold by ten. I continued anyway, putting on my raingear from my pack. First sprinkles, then rain, then hail showers. No place to hide from the pellets pounding the granite boulders, none high enough for shelter, each big enough to be difficult to climb up and over. I was exposed, not a good place to be in a summer thunderstorm.

I sat and waited, motionless, wondering how far I had come. The rock piles on the topo map became five humps up the mountainside, and by my reckoning I was on hump two. Soon the storm passed. Instantly the sky cleared to brilliant blue, the sun melted clusters of hail, steam rose from the damp granite. I looked for tufts of grass and moss to step on, the solidest earth around. Those small flat stones shifted and turned so easily underfoot.

Halfway up the third and steepest hump, I stopped to catch my breath. I had been climbing along the spine about ten feet from the drop-off, where there's less scree, more moss and grass tufts. But I couldn't force myself to walk any closer to the edge. I leaned against a large square boulder, wishing there had been a trail rather than this helter-skelter scrambling up the scree slope.

I looked upwards to check the route. Outlined against the washed blue sky were the forelegs, shoulders, head and curved horns of a mountain sheep not thirty feet above me. Like a National Geographic nature video, a shot from below showing a mountain sheep braced on the edge of a precipice, outlined in majesty. A still shot.

I froze, half-twisting on the granite boulder. The sheep was looking right at me, checking me out, sizing me up. It was frozen too, moving only the eyes. I sent out greeting vibes, amazed. Where had it come from? Could it live on top of this barren rock pile, with nowhere to hide?

The animal was six inches from the drop-off, and I was blocking its descent. I held my breath and slithered sideways amid the boulders, farther away. Pauses. Inhales and exhales. I was breathing, *Don't go away!* But slowly it started down the rock pile above me, picking its way delicately and silently amid the rubble. It stopped about twenty feet from me, slightly above and to the right, still on the very edge of the drop-off.

I kept sending grateful vibes, thinking, *Is this real?* The ankles were so slender, tan gray body so chunky above them. Nose wide and flattened, more like a llama than a deer. Ears erect, sticking out from the head, circled three-quarters of the way around by slender curving horns outlined by blue sky.

Was this a real animal? I was not sure it was a sheep, not like any sheep I had ever seen, the domestic woolly kind we used to raise when I was a kid. Yet it couldn't be a mountain goat, because those horns curved around the ears until they faced forward. Yet the horns were so thin, not massive at all, like the pictures I had seen of rams' heads. I assumed it was a male, from the horns.

That frozen moment in time, a gift, ended as he continued slow-motion down the trail I had missed, his black hooves grafted to the rock. He didn't slip or slide on loose scree. No rocks rolled down the mountain. This inhospitable ground was his territory. He was perfectly at ease here; the scrawny struggling tufts of grass enough. How he must have loved being on top of the world looking all around and down.

Slowly he edged by, occasionally glancing sideways at me, completely silent and poised. The hair was short and dense like a deer's, but the color more buff. The butt was like an antelope, white and flat with a thin black tail bisecting the rump. So chunky, yet tail so delicate. The breeze brought a whiff of damp musk.

About thirty feet below me he stopped and bent down, chewed, and moved on. I watched until he shrank to marmot-size as he continued past humps of rock and rubble below, matching the tan-gray shadings of his granite surroundings. So peaceful.

Our silence ended with a distinct yet distant rasp of metal on granite. I glanced toward the bottom of the mountain. Were other hikers coming? When I looked back, I had lost him. I looked and looked, but he had faded into the granite hillside hundreds of yards below. Yet I knew he was still there, motionless, merged perfectly with his mountain.

Renewed and strengthened, I climbed upwards following his path. It was a trail! I braved the sheer edge without looking down, still clinging to boulders and slithering over scree until I reached the top.

At the summit I was surrounded by dozens of white butterflies fluttering about the gray-white rocks. At the topmost cairn I signed the logbook in the bottle and sat to enjoy the 10,700-foot view. Yet I kept seeing those curved horns, ears and head framed against the sky. What would it be like to come from the mountain top, clear of vision and peaceful of heart? To walk delicately, step by step, undaunted by rubble, unfazed by scree? To nourish myself whenever I came upon a tuft of grass, in however unlikely a spot, and continue peacefully on life's way?

Going back down was quick and easy. I walked upright, hands outstretched for balance. I walked delicately, slowly, steadily, sure amidst rock and rubble. On the trail, which had been there the whole time, at the edge. I had gained a sense of balance in that shifting terrain.

Later that evening, around a campfire, I shared this experience with park rangers. They told me no mountain sheep had been sighted in this wilderness since 1981, and then only by the resident wilderness ranger, with binoculars, at 300 yards. Some were envious; some around the campfire didn't believe me.

One said, "It's amazing he came so close!"

"Well, he had to get by on the trail," I said.

They all laughed. "He could have bounded away, easily, in any direction, if he'd wanted to. Or vanished before you even looked up."

The rangers told me the small curved horns indicated either a young male or a solitary female. I decided she was female.

Yes, she certainly hadn't needed to come closer, nor inched by me against the drop-off. I began to realize that, according to native tradition, she was also a spirit animal. I had seen her up close from all directions: head on, from before, from the side, from the rear, from above. And we had stared at each other; locked glances. From her that day I've acquired a delicate balance, a poise of Spirit, to walk through the rubble of our civilization. George Fox had his Pendle Hill, and I've had my Little's Peak experience.

Dorothy Mack *is a member of Corvallis Friends Meeting (Oregon).*
(*What Canst Thou Say?* April 1996)

~ ~ ~ ~ ~ ~ ~ ~ ~ ~ ~ ~ ~

Snakes, Orchids, and Novels

William R. Stimson

I set out at a young age to be a naturalist. I grew up out in the back country on the Isle of Pines, Cuba, and spent my free time there trekking into the wild to collect native orchids. I was the youngest member of the Cuban Orchid Society, and by the age of 13 was credited with the discovery of a new species—*Oncidium intermedium*. I took it up to Havana myself to deliver it to the famous Richard Evans Schultes, who was down from Harvard University. And so I figured I knew what I was doing a year or two after the Cuban revolution, when exiled in Miami, Florida, I got my first chance to go back out into the wilds.

I was at Southwest Miami High. An acquaintance had a car and was interested in wild orchids. I assured him I could find him orchids if he would just take me out into the Everglades. After all, in my mind I was an expert and knew everything there was to know about finding orchids in the wild. I became a kind of Daniel Boone when I hit the woods. I was in my element. My acquaintance, in contrast, was a city boy. When we finally parked the car off the Loop Road that in those days cut down off the bend in the Tamiami Trail at a point deep in the wilderness, it was humorous to see how hesitantly he stepped off the dirt road into the vegetation. As for myself, I just burst into foliage and left my befuddled companion far behind.

Although I was wearing tennis shoes—a big no-no when you're in snake country—I lit out at a full run behind a huge black snake I spotted. After all, I was carrying my Cuban machete with me. I figured I could handle myself. I couldn't keep up with the snake, though. It slithered faster than I could run. In the end I gave up and set off looking for orchids again. I had never been in a cypress head before and so was fascinated. I was traveling fast and I was traveling alone. My companion still hadn't caught up with me. That's when I spotted the orchids.

I had come to the edge of a clearing, maybe some thirty or forty feet across. On the opposite side was an old rotten tree festooned with epiphytic orchids. Filled with pride that I hadn't lost my touch, I yelled out to my companion, "Orchids. Millions of orchids!" and lit out blindly across that clearing, never taking my eyes off the orchids. I was half-way across the clearing when an alarm went off in my mind. *Snake!*

I was standing with one leg in the air, about to step over a log directly in my path. The only thing I can figure is that I had always known two things about snakes: (1) never wear tennis shoes into snake country because most fatal snake bites occur below the ankle, and (2) never step over a log, as there may be a snake curled up on the other side of it. Hurriedly, I cast a cursory glance down at the log to make sure it was safe. Lying on the other side of the log, right where I was about to put my foot, was a venomous snake with the big triangular head of a pit viper.

I froze there, poised on one foot, beginning to lose my balance. The ground was muddy and wet, slippery. I went to step back but in horror yanked my foot back up in the air. There was an identical snake right behind me. I lost my balance and, so as not to topple over, leapt up onto the log. It was a short little log and began to wobble back and forth in the mud. A third snake crawled out from the log. When I looked down in horror at it, I saw there was a fourth one next to it. And a fifth! And a sixth! The entire open area between me and the orchids, I now saw, as I actually looked at the ground for the first time, was covered with deadly water moccasins.

It was not a clearing at all I had rushed into so blindly, but a dried-up pond—probably the last one in this whole region to go dry just before the onset of the rainy season. All the snakes from the swamp miles and miles around had become concentrated here. They lay criss-crossed every which way, tangled over one another, eating the shiny silver minnows that covered the mud. This was their last feast of the season. By then, I was waving my arms to keep my balance on the log that kept spinning one way then the other in the mushy mud.

I managed to turn around on the log with a mind to get back out of there, only to find the snakes were just as thick in the direction I had come from. The sight of so many water moccasins (cottonmouths), with their big triangular heads, made me queasy. At that point my friend appeared at the edge of the dried-up pond. He just stood there staring. His jaw dropped.

I wasn't the intrepid explorer from Cuba anymore. I was a terrified teenager in tennis shoes trying like a lumberjack to keep his balance on a slippery log right plumb in the middle of several hundred deadly cottonmouths. Then, that boy vanished and something that had more sense than he did carefully stepped off the log and right into the middle of the nearest footprint in the mud.

It was only then, as I stepped carefully and slowly back, retracing my exact steps through the snakes, that I noticed how caught up they were in eating their minnows. They really weren't too interested in me. Had I stepped on one in my mad and blind rush for the orchids, I would surely have been dead. But I could see now, tiptoeing my way cautiously back through the snakes, that my footsteps had fallen exactly in those rare open spots of mud between the snakes. There were so many snakes and they were so thick that they criss-crossed over each other. And yet, without even looking down—my eyes had been fixed on the orchids the whole time—I hadn't stepped on a single snake.

By the time I got to where my companion was waiting safely at the edge of the dried-up pond, I was badly shaken up and had no more taste for exploration that day. I just headed slowly and cautiously back for the road, without any orchids.

I gave little thought to the events of that day until a great many years later. I was much older and completing a Ph.D. in biology at Columbia University when I realized I didn't want to be a scientist. Surrounded by biophysicists, biochemists and the like, I knew quite a bit about phyto-chrome physiology, especially as it related to cyclic photophosphorylation and anthocyanin synthesis—but it had begun to dawn on me: none of this had the least bit to do with who I was, what I was about. I had begun reading novels that dealt with human nature, in the deepest sense of that word. I realized it was this I was interested in exploring, more than biology, more than the wilderness. I felt it to be, at least in my case, in more immediate need of healing.

Suddenly I saw the obvious: the only way to heal nature on the outside is to heal our own inner nature. It's our disturbed heart—our wrong values—that's wrecked the integrity of every single ecosystem on earth. I got my Ph.D. degree, but a few years later gave up my profession as a biology professor and took a weekend job waiting on tables at an Italian restaurant. I set out to become a novelist. The years went by, though, and the "big novel" never materialized. I lost the waiter job. I lost the woman I loved. I was destitute. I still saw no evidence I had any talent for writing. Once again, I had rushed headlong forward and gotten myself into a predicament of danger. It was then I remembered the episode of the snakes.

It occurred to me for the first time how utterly impossible it would have been, statistically, to walk blindly through so many snakes without stepping on a single one. It couldn't have been coincidence. Something had to have been guiding my steps that day in the swamp until it could get my notice and get me safely back out of there. That something—call it what you will—how can we know what it is—was still leading me on. This is what I realized.

It dawned on me that where my life was going probably had as little to do with novels as it did with orchids. My life, I began to see, had everything to do with that which was deepest in my own nature and which saw what I didn't and knew what I couldn't. It was that I had found my first intimations of, in the Big Cypress Swamp so many decades ago—not orchids. And it was that to which I was finding my way closer by turning away from science towards art, away from the mind towards the heart—not novels.

To walk its path as my own is my goal now and, to the extent I have been able to accomplish this on a day-by-day basis over the years, my life has become richer by far than I ever could have imagined—woman or no woman; money or no money; success or no success.

What I have found is so much more beautiful and powerful than anything that profession or position has to offer. To the extent I enter into contact with that incorruptible core within, I have more by far to give the human world than that world could ever possibly have to give me.

If we can only turn around in time and come in whatever way possible, as individuals or collectively, somehow closer to what is deepest and truest in our nature, we can leave our children a healthier planet than the one left to us. This is what it means now—at least to me—to be a naturalist. We have to start with ourselves.

William R. Stimson *now lives in Taiwan. More of his writing can be found at* <*www.my-hope.com/Bill*>.

(This was originally published in *What Canst Thou Say?* in February 1999 "Nature," then later modified and published in *Snowy Egret* and *Pilgrimage*.)

~~~~~~~~~~~~~

Focusing on the Experience

Ken Tapp

For me, nature photography is a spiritual hobby. The world is a sacred place and a sacred process. And I feel fully attentive and intimately involved in that sacred process when I am observing nature with my camera.

Almost every time I take my camera into the woods for a hike, or even just out to my flower garden for a closer look, three things happen. First, I become a better observer; I begin to see things I have previously ignored; I begin to see familiar things in new ways. Secondly, I become aware that nature is always posing for me; and I sense that these poses are manifestations of the Divine spirit—evidence of the sacredness of the world around me. And thirdly, if I stay long enough, or pause quietly enough, I often feel that I am involved in prayer.

But the feeling doesn't fit the definition of prayer that I grew up with: kneel down—bow your head—fold your hands—and talk out loud to some "God" out there somewhere. Rather, the feeling fits a personal definition of prayer I created for myself at a Northern Yearly Meeting workshop on spiritual discipline a few years ago: *Prayer is taking the time to connect with the presence of the Divine around us and within us— pausing long enough to connect with the sacredness, to feel a part of it.* That's what prayer is for me. And that's what happens to me when I spend time trying to photograph nature.

I use nature as my window to the Divine. When I observe nature, I see example after example of the sacredness around me. When I observe nature, I see evidence of continuing revelation. And, if I'm really mindful and fully attentive, I feel myself participating in the prayer of life.

The problem comes in trying to share or explain that experience. I used to think I could share my experience when I shared my photographs. As Ansel Adams said, "Photography is a way of telling people what you feel about what you see." If I feel the Divine, if I feel the sacredness, if I feel the prayer, then surely that should come through if my photos are good enough. But I no longer think it works that way. I think there can be something missing when I show you my photographs. They come from my experience, not yours—unless you've had a similar experience.

Poets and painters often observe nature. Many of them sense the Divine; they experience the prayer. Poets share what they feel with words penned on paper, and perhaps read aloud. Painters show us what they feel with brushstrokes on canvas. But sometimes there's something missing when I read their poems or look at their paintings. The artistic product is about the artist's experience, not necessarily mine. The extent to which the poem or painting does describe an experience I've also had has a lot to do with how meaningful that artist's rendition is for me.

I never really feel like I'm creating a photograph of nature. Rather, I'm experiencing, attempting to record, and then to share what the Divine creates for me, with me, through me. It's the experience that counts, not the picture I hang on my wall. When I take a picture of a bee on a flower, my spiritual experience is no less important and no less meaningful than the spiritual experience Ansel Adams had when he used skills I couldn't begin to match to take his most famous photographs. And, my experience is no more important or no more meaningful than the experience the 10-year old girl has when she excitedly uses her little disposable camera to take a distant, blurry, underexposed picture of a deer she sees beside the road. Each of us experiences our own personal prayer. And that experience counts far more than the product we use to record it.

Ken Tapp is a member of the Beloit Friends Meeting (Wisconsin). Nature is always posing for him, wherever he may be. He is married to WCTS editor Kathy Tapp.

(*What Canst Thou Say?* May 2002 "Arts and the Spirit")

~ ~ ~ ~ ~ ~ ~ ~ ~ ~ ~ ~

Patience

Carmen Bruce

I drove through a shower
of golden leaves, falling
like fresh winter
snow.
I sat and listened to
the honking geese
migrating overhead.
In the distance, I heard
the buzz of the
weed whacker motor
and nearby
the sounds of passersby.
In all this motion
sat I
learning to wait for the
Butterfly.

Carmen Bruce is a member of Providence Friends Meeting (Pennsylvania). She lives as much as possible in the present moment, where she writes her poetry.

(*What Canst Thou Say?* August 2003 "Celebration and Thanksgiving")

God in Times
of Pain and Despair

The more helpless and poverty stricken we are when we turn to God for
aid, the deeper we enter into God and the more sensitive we become to God's
most precious gifts.[13]   —Meister Eckhart (1260–1327)

(*What Canst Thou Say?* February 2000
"Wholeness in the Midst of Brokenness")

In the midst of the most difficult of times, we can be carried by insight, guidance and a sense of God's presence and power. Our writers struggle with issues of sexual abuse, mental illness, unremitting pain, and deep remorse, and their struggles become filled with Light. They know some problems don't go away, no matter how hard we pray.

But they stop praying for a cure and instead pray for help listening to God's guidance. Nancy Whitt grieves the loss of her almost-ten-year-old niece in "Healing from Hurts," and learns that, although the bottom of her soul has been scraped, she is now able to reach out to others experiencing deep sorrow. Scientist Jay Mittenthal ("Rooted in God") prays to become a vessel of God's peace, and it is so. Demaris Wehr in "A Decision Made from Deep Within" gives over her little daughter's life-threatening illness into God's care, and her daughter is restored to complete health. In "Standing on Holy Ground" Rita Varley prays at the bedside of a dying stranger, and is a witness to his passing from life to death.

In our weakness we can open ourselves for God's creative powers to work a new life in us—a life in which our weakness becomes a gift, which we give back to God and other people. Dimitri Mihalas suffers deep anguish and learns God carries him in his despair ("Depression Is a Gift"). In "Discovering God as Companion" Allison Randall suffers the repeated aftershocks of sexual abuse, but she suffers in the presence and healing power of God. In "ruined"

Kate S. Ahmadi, also a victim of sexual abuse, declares, "I am healing, you are healing, we are healing" in a triumph of spirit over deep wrong.

In this section a number of people share the Light they have received on the dark journey. In "Deciding Not to Pray" Mariellen Gilpin shares her wrenching decision to stop praying so she can heal—and her abiding faith that God is with her in the depths of mental illness. Linda Theresa ("In the Heart of Pain") is challenged to say to her pain, "I love you and am grateful for you," and is able to relax into the pain and fall into a healing sleep. She receives a gift, not in spite of her struggle, but because of it. As part of her growth in "My Cup Runneth Over" Kat Griffith not only stops yelling at her daughter but comes to see God in a new way. There is much to celebrate in the riches of the people who share their stories of God's presence in the hardest of times.

~~~~~~~~~~~~~

Healing from Hurts

Nancy Whitt

When she was almost ten, I lost my niece, Ann Marie. We were soulmates from the day she was born—I walked laps around the house with her on my shoulder when she cried. I heard her say her first word ('bird'), introduced her to poetry, feminist spirituality, and to the cookie store; she introduced me to the wonders of rocks and dogwood blossoms. She and I were joint parents of Sojourner Truth, a black Chihuahua, nicknamed Soji, whom we rescued from animal adoption. For years we sang our special songs in the car when I picked her up from day care or school. I also sang lullabies as I rocked her for hours. Nobody else would listen to me sing, but when I tried to put Ann Marie in bed, she would say "rock-rock" asking me to continue.

At a deep level, we did not know we were not immediate family, and when Ann Marie's mother got a job in Iowa, reality struck. Ann Marie said to me as she was facing the move, "You help me be my *self*." The grief for both of us, mixed with fear and anger, is impossible to describe. I know experientially what it feels like to have a child ripped away. The family dysfunction involved, which did not allow for open expressions of grief except with each other, made things worse.

Ann Marie's healing was a long, difficult process, and is her story to tell. How did I heal? I could not have done it without Shirley, my Quaker women's group, and a nurse who used touch therapy. Shirley was a wise older counselor, who told me it was OK to share my grief with Ann Marie; my allowing myself to show tears, without overwhelming her with the depth of my feelings, allowed her to cry in my arms when she was not allowed to express her sadness to anyone else. Coincidentally, Shirley's daughter had died at the time Ann Marie was leaving, and we shared rage and grief with each other, not fearing to express whatever feelings we had, including a fantasy of machine-gunning everyone in her church on Easter Sunday. Having someone understand so deeply helped.

At times, I could not go on. There's the Christian story, which had seemed sort of maudlin, about one set of footprints in the sand because Jesus was carrying the narrator of the story when s/he couldn't do it for her/himself. That's what the Birmingham Friends women's group did for me. I could let myself spiritually rest in them, as if they had formed a web with their arms I could lie in. Meeting each Sunday night in my apartment, they were empathetic and affirming, playing the role also of my reality checks—my feelings were appropriate to the loss.

Finally, at yearly meeting I asked the nurse Sharon Annis for a therapeutic touch session. She discovered in my throat a terribly clogged place, my grief that I couldn't let out, that would have come out in howls of anguish. Her care was soothing and healing. Later, when I underwent a physical procedure concerning a heart valve, as I was coming out of the anesthetic, the image of Sharon appeared as the Goddess looking out for me.

For me, God/dess is immanent. S/he comes through others. I had been saved throughout childhood by always having one person, family or not, seeing *me* alive on the planet. I've had older friends treating me with such love and care, I've had to catch my breath. I've had children to hug and be taught by and to laugh with. I've had older Quaker sisters who drew out of me strengths, talents and skills I didn't know I had. I still have elderly aunts who celebrate me as a young person (even though I'm almost 60). I have a loving daughter who is becoming a beautiful woman. I have good friends, young nephews and nieces—all who bring that of God in themselves to share with me. That's what heals my spirit and keeps it alive and joyful. I believe it also keeps my body healthy—it keeps my body needing to go where the spirit leads it.

Twelve years later, there will always be part of me who lost an almost 10-year-old girl, a woman of sorrows acquainted with grief. Ann Marie, now a loving, creative young woman at the beginning of her adult life, and I remain soulmates, despite large gaps between times we've seen each other. We e-mail and speak on the phone, and she visits me each year.

While none of us seeks hardship, once the bottom of your soul has been scraped, you know how deep you go, and you use your experience when others need the benefit of it—as Shirley and I helped heal each other, I know I've been a healing presence as others have been asked to bear the unbearable. I know now that deeply living, deeply loving is both joyful and painful—I choose to dwell in that very human, very spiritual depth.

 Nancy Whitt *is an aunt and mother who enjoys the roles and enjoys writing personal essays for Quaker publications.*

(*What Canst Thou Say?* November 2003 "Spiritual Healing")

~~~~~~~~~~~~~~

And My Cup Runneth Over

Kat Griffith

"Here we go again," I thought, as I heard Savannah coming down the stairs. I braced myself for our morning encounter, forced a cheerful tone into my voice, and said, "How are you today, honey?"

As expected, she responded with a snarl, followed by a tantrum. My initial attempts to be loving, patient and compassionate soon gave way to rage at her intransigent surliness, and I banished her from the kitchen. While she sobbed in the living room, I fought back tears as I washed the dishes.

What was going on? Why did mornings start out like this? What was I doing wrong? How was it that we had managed so perfectly to reproduce the typical morning scene of my childhood, when every conscious intention on my part was to do different, to do better? I had wanted to be a parent more than anything else in the world; I had waited a long time for it, and finally I had my chance—and here we were starting off our day with this toxic brew of hurt and anger whose origins I simply could not fathom.

I am sitting in a therapist's office, trying to understand the interaction that has poisoned our mornings for months. The therapist has just asked me what, at the moment when Savannah comes down, I really want. I am startled to realize that I have an intense, almost overwhelming yearning for someone to take care of me, to make me a cup of tea, to hold me on their lap. *Suddenly I have a vision of myself as a small child, actually a miniature version of the adult me, in a bathrobe and holding a cup of tea, sitting on... no, there is no lap. The lap I want to be sitting on simply doesn't exist.*

The image of me suspended in air above the hoped-for but nonexistent lap is so bleak I can hardly stand it. This horrible vision haunts me for 36 hours. They are the worst 36 hours of my life.

It seems clear that my own unmet needs make it impossible for me to meet the needs of my morning-cranky child. She sets me off because she reminds me of how I was at the age of five, and she reminds me of what I didn't get. My rage isn't really at her; it is rage at my parents. And it seems that there is no resolving that rage.

I think, "How can I give what I didn't get? How can I offer loving nurturance to my children if I didn't receive it myself? My cup is empty. I don't have it in me to meet their needs. Am I even fit to be a parent?"

Thirty-six hours after the talk with the therapist, I am sitting in the living room at dawn, doing my daily spiritual practice. I am crying and praying, asking God to rescue me from my darkness and make me the mother I want to be. Suddenly, I look to the other end of the couch and *I see myself, a child-sized version again, in my bathrobe and holding a cup of tea. I am sitting on a lap, only it isn't exactly a lap, it's a brilliant white light. I realize that I feel held, I feel warm, I feel supported and embraced.*

The vision is so real I can touch it. I realize that I am literally sitting "in the Light," on the Light, held by the Light. And I am filled with the realization that it doesn't matter at all what happened in my childhood, God's love now is enough for me. The love I give my children doesn't have to originate in my limited being, it comes from God, and can flow through me to my children and whomever else is in my life. My ability to love my family doesn't depend on my wholeness. It is not limited by my brokenness. It is limited only by my acceptance, or lack of it, of God's love.

I write about the experience in only a few sentences in my journal, and yet it is utterly life-changing. I can't explain exactly how or why, but within two weeks the morning tantrums are over. Completely. I suspect that nothing originating in my will or conscious intention could have achieved this. My attempts to squeeze more (insincere) compassion, and (false) patience out of myself were demonstrably unsuccessful. In the end, the only thing that worked was for me to be so desperate, so destitute of hope, so empty of faith in myself, that there was room in my heart for God.

I think I understand now what it is to be born again. And I think I must be the luckiest mom in the world to have had a tantrum-prone five-year-old, because it was Savannah's tantrums that led the way out of my darkness and into God's light.

Kat Griffith *is a member of Ripon Worship Group (Wisconsin). Now Savannah is 7, Bjorn is 4, and mornings are almost always cuddly and cheerful.*

(*What Canst Thou Say?* August 2002 "God's Marvelous Workarounds")

God is...

Diane Barounis

The breaths we breathe each day
Taking in and giving up—

The Ocean of Light
Bearing us on pregnant waves—

The one true voice that tells us
I will never leave you—

The opening that is created
When the former path gives way—

The strength that makes possible
Every broken-hearted Yes—

The beauty that imbues all that is
Just as it is—

The love that remains when shattered souls
Can no longer bear to love—

In the searing
Cries of war—

In the holy shadows
Of prayers unspoken—

In every uninhabitable
And unloved place—

In death
And through death—

God is—
With us always
Amen.

Diane Barounis *is a member of Evanston Friends Meeting (Illinois). She is a clinical social worker and envisions this poem as a prayer.*

(*What Canst Thou Say?* November 2002 "Spiritual Metaphors")

Depression is a Gift

Dimitri Mihalas

I slipped into a major depression in September of 1985. By December, I dropped very suddenly into a suicidal state. In early January, 1986, I went home one afternoon to pull the trigger. But my wife had already removed the gun from the house, and my plan was thwarted. Being incapacitated to the point I could not immediately come up with another plan, I was stuck, and I simply stumbled forward as well as I could.

Somewhere during the end of January or early February, my wife and I had lunch near campus. In walking back we parted company to go to our respective offices. It was snowing moderately. I went along for a few steps, and on impulse turned around to look at her going away. As she moved further along her path, I watched her slowly disappear into the falling snow: first her white knit cap, then her parka, then… gone! In an instant I felt a tremendous pang of loneliness, a tremendous sense of loss and emptiness as I found myself asking, "What would happen if she suddenly disappeared? How could I stand it? How would I survive?" Then a very short time later I understood that those terrible questions would be hers if I were to kill myself. I felt like I had been hit with both barrels of a shotgun.

What I eventually came up with is that my life isn't really mine. It belongs to me, sure, but in the context of all the other lives it touches. And that when all the chips are down on the table, I don't have the moral/ethical right to destroy my life because of the impact that would have on all the people who know and love me. Killing myself implies killing part of them. I could understand very clearly that I did not want any of the people I love killing themselves. By reciprocity I realized they would say the same of me, and at that moment I recognized the only morally and ethically acceptable path open to me was to hang on as long as I possibly could.

Sometime later, I no longer know exactly when, I experienced a delayed reaction to the event described above. While part of my mind was still bent on suicide, and had to be resisted, in another part of my mind I felt an increasingly strong conviction that I was being protected, sheltered, and that it would all come out all right. It helped to quiet my worst fears; it offered the faintest breath of hope even though my depression was as severe as ever. I felt that I had been touched. I can't say for sure that it was God who touched me, though that seems a valid metaphor for the experience, but I know for certain that it was a force of tremendous power, and that the merest touch of it is enough to last a lifetime.…

[In the summer of 1993] in the Boulder Meeting I was thinking back to 1986/87, and the pure hell I went through then; how painful it was, how crushing and frightening. I found myself asking, "Was that a test? Was it punishment? Was it a trial?" And then I remembered that it was then that I first felt touched (by God's hand?), felt guided, held, carried, protected, even in the deepest darkest places. So I had to conclude it simply couldn't be a test or punishment; that wouldn't make sense. So I asked again, "Why is it given to us to have to travel through such terrible darkness?"

Suddenly I knew the answer! It is a child's answer: so obvious that only a child might ever think of it. It is this: *it is in the deepest darkness that one can most easily see light, God's Light, your Inner Light.* As an astronomer, let me say something else obvious: if you want to see stars, you don't go out at noon. You go out at midnight. And the darker it is then, the more, and fainter, stars you can see. The picture I got is that in our lives, our Inner Light may get obscured, covered over by all kinds of things such as pride, anger, arrogance, greed, betrayal, false belief, illness, pain… on and on. Eventually there comes the day when we can't see it any more. Then we are lost, yet only we can find ourselves again. But then if we are plunged into great darkness, we have a chance to find that Light again, no matter how faint it might have become. So I was led to the amazing conclusion that the dark journey is not a test, a trial, or a punishment, it is a gift!

Dimitri Mihalas *is a member of Boulder Friends Meeting (Colorado). "Thanks to my illness, I have almost died 4 times. I now know the light never fails, and one need merely reach out to feel God's touch."*

(Excerpted from *Depression and Spiritual Growth*, Pendle Hill Pamphlet #327 in *What Canst Thou Say?* February 2000 "Wholeness in the Midst of Brokenness")

~~~~~~~~~~~~~

I had been meditating on my state in great depression. I seemed to hear the words articulated in my spirit, "Live up to the light thou hast, and more will be granted thee."[14]   —Caroline Fox (1819–1871)

(*What Canst Thou Say?* November 2000 "Visions and Voices")

~~~~~~~~~~~~~

A Decision Made from Deep Within

Demaris Wehr

In my experience, effective intercessory prayer is characterized by the deepest level of desire, truthfulness and intent one can muster. In my own case, it has sometimes been a prayer prayed in agony and anguish; at other times, prayer has been accompanied by an extraordinary peace. But in all cases, when it's "worked," it has been characterized by a decision made from deep within, and never from a neutral, indifferent, repetitious or bored place.

Probably my first intercessory prayer, ever, was one made on my own behalf. It was a time of great mental, emotional and spiritual suffering. I was young and desperately unhappy, feeling trapped in my first marriage. My parents had undergone an unbelievably confusing and traumatic divorce a few years earlier. This had no doubt catapulted me into my marriage as a remedy for the pain caused by the divorce.

My husband and I had recently become parents of a dear little girl who was sick a lot. My husband had a clear sense of his identity and calling. He had recently been appointed as a junior faculty member at Haverford College, while I was a "mere housewife." He worked constantly, it seemed, while my talents lay fallow as I took care of Kirsten (or so it felt to me at the time). My self-esteem was at an all-time low. The women's movement hadn't yet made its appearance. I was suffering from "battle fatigue" (by which I mean the ongoing, unresolved trauma of my parents' very difficult divorce) and from the unnamable syndrome from which many educated young mothers suffered in the 1960s. I remember walking across the sun-filled Haverford campus one afternoon in desperation. My first intercessory prayer was: "Dear God, if You exist, help me."

To my amazement, this prayer worked. Over time, though not immediately, things began showing up in my life that had not been there before. That simple prayer had the elements of what I have come to identify in effective prayer. It was heartfelt. It was honest. There was a deep intent to get better, to get out of the mess I was in, though I had absolutely no idea how. That prayer obviously had an intensity that is somewhat unusual, for I remember it still. I have prayed many prayers since, but many of them are forgotten. That one is remembered.

A few years later found me divorced, living alone in Ann Arbor with my then four-year-old daughter. The next incident of prayer changed my life. It happened this way. My daughter was prone to convulsions, which terrified me. She had spent a week in Children's Hospital in Philadelphia undergoing a battery of tests to determine their cause. The test results were inconclusive, leaving me with no recourse but phenobarbitol, baby aspirin and panic-stricken cool baths in the middle of the night if she had a fever. Unfortunately, she had fevers frequently. The doctors had said she could suffer some brain damage if she had any more convulsions.

One night, Kirsten got a high fever and showed all the signs of an approaching convulsion. A good friend, a Christian Scientist, encouraged me to call a Christian Science practitioner for prayer help for her. We had experienced some minor healings by prayer before this time, so the idea didn't seem totally foreign to me. I called the practitioner, who assured me that Kirsten was fine and in God's care. This seemed weird to me. How could she be fine? But this man was so certain, and spoke from such a depth of conviction, that he got my attention. After hanging up, rather than running for the phenobarbitol, as had been my habit, I sat down and prayed. I also read a portion of Mrs. Eddy's book, *Science and Health*.[15]*

Not long after, I went downstairs to check on Kirsten. Nothing had changed. Her breathing was rapid and shallow; her skin was hot to the touch. Normally, upon observation of symptoms such as these, my heart would start racing and I would literally run for the medicine and start running the bath. I would wake up my sleepy daughter, plunge her, protesting, into the cool water, try to distract her with toys while she railed about, wanting out of the water. This time, however, my state of mind was entirely different. It was not exactly an altered state of consciousness, although it was certainly not my habitual state of consciousness in that situation.

What happened next was a deep moment of reckoning. I stood next to Kirsten's bed listening to her breathe. The practitioner had said she was fine. As I stood there, I asked myself: "Do I believe in God or not?" I made myself vote. I waited, in silence, for the deepest truth of me to emerge. Finally, I answered "yes" to my question. *Something* sank deeper in me.

Then I asked myself: "Do I trust the practitioner or not?" Again, I stood there and made myself be absolutely honest. No fudging here. From the depths of my being arose an affirmation. "Yes, he seems honest; as people go, remarkably honest." *Something* sank even deeper.

Next, I stood there and addressed God—the God I hadn't even known existed in my prayer of two years earlier, and about whom I had only become sure in the preceding five minutes. "God," I said, "I'm terrified, but I leave her with you." And I turned around and walked out of her bedroom. Soon thereafter, I fell into a peaceful sleep in my own bed.

---

* Please note this is not a plug for Christian Science. This is merely an honest description of what happened. It was highly unusual, as you will see. The power behind this healing is the property of no denomination. It has to be accessible to all or it couldn't be accessible to any.

Imagine my amazement as, the next morning, four-year-old, golden-haired Kirsten came bounding up the stairs fully healed. I felt as though I stood on sacred ground, totally new terrain. My daughter was healed (and by the way, she never had another convulsion; never even came close). Even more importantly, my worldview had shifted to one which now included a good, loving God with actual capability of healing disease. For the first time in years, I felt safe. And joy-filled. My daughter was safe. This conviction of fundamental, existential safety undergirded my prayers from that time on. And my prayers became increasingly effective as a result, I think, of my deepened faith.

Dear friends, I do not know how to conclude this article. There is a tension to hold, it seems to me, between experiences like mine above and those painful ones where prayer seems to go unanswered. I do know that when I've really gotten "down there," as I tried to describe, healings happened. However, there have been times when I couldn't get there; when I tried and tried and tried to the point of obsession with no luck. How does one find a graceful combination of surrender and hope? How does one find the ability to live with what is, if what is, is ongoing suffering? I do not know the answers to these questions. I only know that help has come my way as a result of deep prayer, and that now, prayer itself, regardless of results is, for me, a sustaining activity.

Demaris Wehr *is a Jungian psychotherapist. Summers she goes to Bosnia with the Karuna Center for Multicultural Transformation and Peacebuilding..*

(*What Canst Thou Say?* August 2000 "Called to Intercessory Prayer")

~ ~ ~ ~ ~ ~ ~ ~ ~ ~ ~ ~ ~

About a dozen years ago I became critically ill and I have a vivid memory of looking down on my self on the bed; doctors and nurses worked on that body, and I felt held in such sureness, joy and contentment and sense of the rightness of things....The crisis passed and I was filled with wonder at the newness of life....There were times when truly out of the depths I cried; I had no reserves of strength left, either physical, emotional or spiritual, but I never completely lost the memory of being held and the wonder at being alive. Gradually the wounds healed; old griefs as well as disease and operations.[16]
—Jennifer Faulkner, 1982

(*What Canst Thou Say?* November 2000 "Spiritual Healing")

In the Heart of Pain

Linda Theresa

Too weak to hold my head up, too exhausted to think rationally, I still couldn't sleep. Every muscle, every organ screamed in painful anguish. The doctors said I would probably be in pain many weeks or many months. Not wanting to be a junkie, I decided to avoid painkillers; besides, I felt the pain must be trying to tell me something. Excruciating pain seemed endless. I did what most people in my position would do—I prayed. "Please tell me what to do. I don't know why this is happening. Please, please help me. I am open to any message. I'm willing to try anything."

Groveling. Isn't it amazing how pain cuts through stubbornness? Surprisingly, when I'm willing to see and try anything, I always seem to get answers, never of the sort I might expect. I expect to hear something like, "It's okay, Linda, you don't need to do anything." Instead the answers challenge me.

This time, when sleep at long last rescued me, directions came in a woman's soothing voice. Who says dreams can't be specific? This one was a virtual instruction manual. The instructions were so simple, the benefits so profound. Yet to this day, I struggle to follow them. Here is the four-step plan she gave me:

1) Gently and openly, become aware of all thoughts and sensations.

2) Love whatever comes up. (You got it, even the pain.)

3) Learn self-control.

4) Put what you've learned into action.

When I awoke, her reassurance and hope inspired immediate action. I settled down to watch the severe pain. Swollen muscles hurt intensely and small spasms flitted through them. Joints ached. Swollen throat throbbed. The diaphragm unwillingly labored to allow shallow gasps of air. Trying to sit up caused racing heart and dizzy exhaustion. The medical profession called this "Chronic Fatigue Syndrome."

After awhile, I noticed an increase in pain. Hmmm. What was that little fleeting thought just before the pain increased? Yes, I had thought, "I am uncomfortable." Wow, did that thought have anything to do with my pain level increasing? I didn't want to hear the answer. I got angry instead. What am I supposed to do if I can't even think how I feel? Just answer me that one, God.

My anger faded as I remembered the loving inspiration of the dream. I decided to go on with step two: Love whatever comes into awareness. At the time it never occurred to me that my thought was what came into awareness. My pain took center stage. It was all I could think about, so I focused on loving it. This proved to be a task requiring massive effort.

Before now, I had always tried to distract my mind from the pain. I wanted to suppress knowing about it. I definitely wanted to suppress feeling it. The dream promised a way out. Being able to muster up a sincere, "Pain, I love you and I'm grateful for you," took a half hour of concentration and struggle. When I succeeded, the pain lessened and I immediately fell into a deep, healing sleep.

You would think I had have mastered this process over many months in and out of severe pain. Yet it took three years before I could say it with enough conviction that my body became totally relaxed and my mind totally open. Thoughts of discomfort quit plaguing me as I focused on the perfection of God. This only happened once, but that once defied all expectation.

I've heard about rare cases of women in childbirth having an experience like this. It didn't make any sense to me, mostly because they couldn't find words adequate enough to describe what had happened. Now, here I am trying to tell you what words cannot capture. Only one word rang through my mind—*glorious*. I felt I was in the presence of God as part of the ongoing pain for, perhaps, a half-hour. The pain subsided with the experience. I tried to write about it in my journal, but writing seemed as ancient as chiseling words into a granite rock. Knowing was enough.

Paradoxically, I am not against the use of painkillers. The rhythm of growth for me involves cycles of change and rest. Painkillers may assist relaxation by lessening pain and fear. Healing and answers often come during these periods of integrative respite.

Pain wakes us up and alerts us to danger. We dislike pain. It motivates us to change and to feel that which is uncomfortable. Like me, you might look at a change in your fundamental beliefs, such as, giving credence to the power of thought and re-directing love of oneself. Watch out! If you try out ideas in this article, you, too, might discover that loving yourself includes accepting and honoring your pain. This price might be worth knowing the heart of pain—glorious, unconditional love.

Linda Theresa *belongs to Wider Quaker Fellowship.*

(*What Canst Thou Say?* May 1998 "Healing")

~ ~ ~ ~ ~ ~ ~ ~ ~ ~ ~ ~

Look inward often, with the desire that others should also scrutinize you and put you to the test.... There is no resting place in this world. That has never existed for anybody, no matter how holy they became.[17]

—Meister Eckhart (1260–1327)

(*What Canst Thou Say?* November 2003 "Birth and Rebirth")

ruined

Kate S. Ahmadi

we hear a speech
childrens law

women and children
go through the
system
criminal justice
system

criminal yes
justice no

conclusion
they are ruined

i too have been put
on trains
holding little
brothers hand
heads exploding
mother waving
goodbye

we reach the door of
that house
brother and i
do not want to open
it
blue door

years later
dear man helps me
walk through that
door
house

living room
dining room
hall
bedroom
bath
sink
tub

white tiles

shaking
moaning
grunting

whimpering
soaked with sweat

an animal
you are an animal
Katie

indian hill
we live on top

delaware lackawanna
and
western tracks
bottom

day

we wave to engineers
they wave back

night

train roars uphill
whoo whoo whoo

ruined
declension
they are ruined
we are ruined
i am ruined

you are right to shun us
the ruined

we are dangerous

feelings
dangerous
damned right

stick to words
mind
safer

do not open that blue door

despair
rage

we want to run
kill
die
dead children yes
but ruined
hell no

they are not ruined
we are not ruined
i am not ruined
you are not ruined

i am healing
we are healing

you are ruined
you who say the word
ruined

leaders

you who label
revictimize us

you who hear the word
ruined

followers

deaf

hear no evil
see no evil
speak no evil

you who wave

children smaller
smaller

whoo whoo whoo

Kate S. Ahmadi *lives on Woodcock Mountain, where she attempts to live the simple life.*

   (*What Canst Thou Say?* August 2002 "God's Marvelous Workarounds")

Standing on Holy Ground

Rita Varley

About a year and a half ago, Barbara, my next door neighbor, invited me to accompany her on a visit to her uncle, who was in a hospital dying of cancer. I had never met her uncle, but was glad to spend some time with Barbara and to be supportive of her. When we came into his room at the hospital there were two other relatives who had not seen Barbara in a while, and they began to visit with her in soft voices. Since I didn't know any of the relatives, I didn't join the conversation. I sat silently in the corner, and turned my attention to the uncle who was lying in the bed, quietly unconscious. I prayed for him, and held him in the Light.

After the hospital visit, Barbara and I returned to our homes. I went to bed around 10:00 and fell asleep. I was awakened suddenly, feeling like I was beside Barbara's uncle, feeling him wiggling back and forth, trying to get loose from his body. I sent him love, and prayed for him. He came loose and I could feel him get free of the body, and all was well. I had no doubt about what I had just experienced, and felt honored to be permitted to participate in the sacrament of his crossing over.

I looked at my clock and saw that it was around 15 minutes after midnight. The next day, Barbara called me in the afternoon to tell me her uncle had been pronounced dead at 12:30 that night.

It was interesting to me to discover how close a connection to a previously unknown person can be created through quiet focused prayer. My attention during prayer had been relaxed and receptive such as when watching a movie. Most of my experiences of spiritual connection with people close to death (either before or after) have been with people not close to me. When the dying person was close to me I was so caught up with the physical aspects and needs of the moment, that they crowded out the relaxed state required to be receptive to non-physical contact.

Rita Varley is a member of Central Philadelphia Friends Meeting (Pennsylvania), has two grown daughters, and is Head Librarian of Philadelphia Yearly Meeting Library.

(*What Canst Thou Say?* February 2003 "Death and Dying")

~~~~~~~~~~~~~~

Keep me ever aware and ever prepared for the summons. If pain comes before the end, help me not to fear it or struggle against it but to welcome it as a hastening of the process by which the strings that bind me to life are untied. Give me joy in awaiting the great change that comes after this life of many changes, grant that my self be merged into Thy Self as a candle's wavering light is caught up into the sun.[18]

—Elizabeth Gray Vining (1902–1999)

(*What Canst Thou Say?* February 2003 "Death and Dying")

~ ~ ~ ~ ~ ~ ~ ~ ~ ~ ~ ~ ~

Discovering God as Companion

Allison Randall

There is a spiritual that goes, "Lord, don't move the mountain, but give me the strength to climb. Please don't move that stumbling block, but give me the strength to go around it." Five years ago an episode of sexual abuse destroyed my personal belief system and my life as it had been. During the five years since, I have sung this spiritual often, alone, as prayer, but with these words: "Lord, please move the mountain, or give me the strength to climb. If you don't move the stumbling block, give me the strength to go around it."

The mountain, the stumbling block, is the heap of residue left from the abuse: fear that comes on me suddenly, triggered by something that reminds my body of the abuse and leaves me with strange results: fear of men, fear of sex, shaking and stuttering, inability to focus my thoughts because they fire off in every direction, an inability to read... and much more. These episodes of fear happen less and less frequently—now maybe once every two months, and now don't last more than a day, but every time they return, I long for the me that used to be.

As I work my way around the stumbling blocks, God is working around them too, with me. Soon after the abuse I was having a dreadful time remembering anything. I was leaving things all over the place, forgetting where I put everything. The fine man who is now my husband said at the time, when I complained about having to run back into my apartment to get something I had forgotten, "You didn't forget, you remembered," emphasizing the positive. And I found myself trying hard to do this all the time—turn things around so I could appreciate the flip side.

I knew now experientially that God was not Protector, but I had come to know God more strongly, deeply, as Companion—Companion who sometimes even took on the face of Christ (who had not previously played a part in my religious beliefs). When I found myself unable to sit quietly in private meditation as I had done for years, I discovered private singing, and found that the appropriate hymns and spirituals would frequently present themselves to me, and singing out loud alone became wonderfully healing prayer. When I could not pray in my accustomed silence without words, I discovered out-loud prayer with words, and when I could not pray out loud with words, I discovered throwing myself on the ground in despairing, pleading prayer with wordless sounds.

Soon after the abuse one of my brothers got me a simple-to-use camera, through which I could choose to see only a small part of the world at a time—small enough that I could deal with. Through the lens I could have complete control over what I saw, and make it as big or as small as I wanted. Each picture I snapped was a prayer of gratitude—for being able to take the picture, for this small amount of control that I needed so much to exercise in my life, for the beauty of whatever I was taking a picture of: the snow at the base of a tree, tree shadows across green grass, the pattern of barn boards around a barn window.

I began to accept my own brokenness as I moved the camera, watching the pictures change as I looked through its lens, finding beauty in collapsing barns and broken windows. As my lens captured the loveliness of shadows on rocks and trees or reflections in bodies of water, shadows and reflections in my own life echoed in my heart.

As I discovered each photograph with my lens and was awed by its beauty—beauty that constantly existed all around me—I had just to take up my camera and look!—my heart leapt in awe at the abundance of beauty in Creation. Each shot became a prayer, flowing easily, springing spontaneously from my overflowing and needy heart: "Thank you, God, for this myriad of wonder" ... "for this incredible cloud formation" ... "for these unbelievable colors" ... "for the impermanence of delicate fern shadows on a solid, seemingly permanent rock." And so this taking of photographs was helping me heal and helping me feel more strongly again the presence, the wonder, of God. And through it God was teaching me about impermanence, teaching me not only to accept it, but to see incredible beauty in it.

As I looked at my finished photographs, they gave me much joy. And when I shared them with others, they were very enthusiastic. I have had two shows of my photographs, and when I put up the shows, I included a piece of writing, telling how the camera and these photographs were helping me heal from abuse. I know this has been of help to others because they tell me so.

Soon after the abuse, in a little shop, in a basket full of hand-carved wooden angels from Nigeria, I found an angel with a knothole where his heart should have been. Because it was the man I had loved most who had abused me, I frequently felt a hole where my heart had been. I cried out with empathy and delight at this tiny wooden wounded healer, who has hung on my wall ever since, reminding me I might still be of use to God.

I do not feel that my weakness has given much back to other people yet besides through my photography. It has with individual women who have been abused: I am now able to understand them much better than I did before my own abuse. When they are manifesting some of the same symptoms I have, I know what they need and how best to help them. I empathize with their feelings and frustrations and anger. I have discovered that there are plenty of people in the world who have suffered in other ways: from physical but nonsexual abuse, or from mental abuse, leaving them with some of the problems I now have. Those people, too, I am now much better able to be with in a meaningful and helpful way.

Until the time of the abuse, I had many male friends. Having grown up with three brothers and no sisters, I had always found males more comfortable to be around. I had found them to have much less pretense than women, and to be far more straightforward and honest, which I liked. After the abuse I was fearful of men: they all seemed potentially dangerous. This threw me into the company of women, or into solitude. I have learned much from being thrown into both those places. In the company of women who have been abused I have found great solace and empathy, understanding and incredibly strong bonds. In solitude I have been able to go further and further into God's and my personal relationship, having hours and hours every day where it's just God and me together. That's been good too.

And in those times alone and with women, God has made it clear He has eventual work for me to do concerning abused women. I don't yet know what, but trust the next step toward that work will be given to me when I am ready. I think my heart is still being prepared for it, and that more healing needs to take place within me before I am strong enough to work with other abused women without being thrown back into a place of fear myself. But I know that I will be given ministry in that area. God has made that clear to me. And when that ministry begins, I bet it will feel that God has come full circle, working through the abuse with me.

Allison Randall *is a member of Keene Worship Group (New Hampshire). She attempts to be aware as much as possible of the ways God might be working in her life, and to be grateful.*

(*What Canst Thou Say?* August 2002 "God's Marvelous Workarounds")

The Gift That Follows Surrender

David Blair

Five years ago I ended an affair and began a painful process of getting to know myself, and then of recreating my marriage. The process goes on: though not painful any more, it remains challenging and surprising. I have learned, and continue to learn, so much about my humanity, the dark sides as well as the light within. I'll share a few stories about moments when my greater knowledge of my weakness became a gift to others, as well as to myself.

I teach English as a Second Language. I was working one day four years ago with an eighth grade Cambodian student who had come from gang life in Lowell, Massachusetts. He was in his own way replaying the terrible civil war and genocide that has so deeply affected his parents' generation, and through them, his own. This boy's life experience was so far from mine that a few years before, I would have found no way to connect to him. Yet now I knew the part of myself that could treat another person as nothing—literally annihilate him or her. I didn't feel so much difference between myself and this eighth grader.

As we talked about the Monkey King, Hanuman, in the epic tale, the Ramayana, he said to me: "Sometimes I know the good monkey in me, sometimes the bad one." I was stunned by the way he said this. For that moment, we were two souls hanging out together. There was no gap between us. We truly understood each other, and it was a precious moment for us both.

Last year I helped to facilitate dialogue groups between Serbs and Muslims in Bosnia; also Serbs and Albanians in Kosovo. I saw people in the "victim" group desperately wanting to have their suffering acknowledged; people in the "perpetrator" group trying desperately to justify and defend their people, to cite past historic grievances rather than accept their share of current responsibility for evil deeds—lest they themselves become evil in their own eyes.

I was able to hold both positions in compassion, as I had been in both. I knew how healing it would be for all if the "perpetrators" could acknowledge and even express sorrow for the suffering their people had caused others, but I knew I could not force this moment. And, as we facilitators helped to hold a safe space for the group, some miracles of healing did happen, a transformation did begin. I would never have been able to hold the space for this process had I not been through my own personal dark night and seen in myself all the characters who sat in the circle.

In the last three years my wife has been through her own dark night, not only the trauma of my affair but then she plunged deep into a terrifying depression—her companion for many years, but never so difficult as three years ago. One day we sat in the sun on our porch, the day as beautiful as I could ask for. I looked at her and saw her face contorted in pain. I turned away—how could she feel so terrible on such a perfect day?

In that moment, I knew that my turning away from her brought me true suffering. Before there was pain, but now there was suffering. As I had learned not to turn away from myself, as God never turned away from me, I found it within myself to be with her no matter what came. I prayed constantly for her healing and accepted that the healing might not come in the way I hoped. My own experience of helplessness, and then of wondrous love surrounding me, gave me the strength and the faith to love her in a way I never had or could have before.

At this time I felt a deep longing to apologize to the man whose wife I had slept with. I wanted to write him a letter, but something didn't feel right. The part of me that still held on to memories, and wanted not only to apologize but to be friendly with him and his wife, was too present. The letter could not have been clean as it must be, though the intention to express my remorse was. I tried to bargain with God, promising to give up something important to me if only I could write the letter. The answer was clear: *No*.

One night I knelt on the road by the marsh below my house. I put my head on the pavement and cried, and told this man how sorry I was, and I felt the energy of the apology flowing out the top of my head. I had never felt anything like this before—and haven't since! I got up and knew that somehow it was complete. Within two weeks a most unexpected event brought me face to face with him, and I was able to make it even more complete. This moment was a gift to both of us, a healing I could never have engineered myself. This experience of my weakness, and the letting go of my desire, allowed me to feel the power of intention—without form, spoken or written—and then to receive the miraculous and unexpected gift that can follow surrender.

Three months ago I found myself in a rage against my wife. I did not vent it at her full force, but she knew I was really angry. I prayed for help, and I quickly found that my anger connected back to my rage at my father for leaving my mother, brother and me. It had to do with not being consulted about something really important to me, not being included, not being valued—Linda's action had triggered all these old hurts. I was shocked to find these places still raw, as I had looked at them deeply four years ago and experienced a profound healing with my father.

I realized then that the pain I felt was true and so was the healing. For the first time I understood what it means for pain, or trauma, to enter the cells and tissues of my body, so that it can persist and be triggered even when forgiveness has been given and received. I pray that God may in time heal those tissues too, and I know that if I carry this pain the rest of my life, it is a beautiful gift to me, for it helps me to be with others who carry pain. The next time I sit with a group of war survivors, or with a friend who is deeply hurt, I will have a larger space to hold them in because of what is not yet healed in me.

David Blair *lives in rural New Hampshire and teaches in the public schools. Between 1985 and 1993 he lived in China, the Philippines and Vietnam. The inner journey of the last years has taken him to even more amazing places.*

(*What Canst Thou Say?* August 2002 "God's Marvelous Workarounds")

~~~~~~~~~~~~~

Rooted in God

Jay Mittenthal

This is a story of loss and rebirth of faith in God. The God I had trusted in childhood prayer became encrusted with unwelcome attributes: my mother told me God would punish me for things she didn't want me to do. Synagogue and Sunday School elaborated this image of a God leading and scourging his chosen people. This was not a God of love for all the world. I grew skeptical of seeking aid and comfort from this heavy-handed figure. I found room to grow in the knowledge of stars and planets, trees and insects—room for curiosity, joy in finding and solving puzzles, and approval for my knowledge at home and in school. Thus, in my heart the love of God fell asleep as the love of science awakened.

In college I majored in physics, then biophysics, as the mysteries of molecular biology entangled my imagination. With my study of evolution came a program: I would understand how it all evolved, and this knowledge would bring me peace and security. The further I pursued this goal, the more elusive it seemed. Knowledge was fragmentary and provisional. Nevertheless, I sought fulfillment in work and family for a quarter of a century. I was an agnostic. I prayed rarely, when in great distress, as when I was lost while hiking or when dealing with my brother's mental illness.

Then came my wake-up call. My wife left me. My children went to college. Doing science was a grand entertainment, but its minutiae did not satisfy my desire for wholeness and belonging. I did not want to grow old as my parents had, hiding despair behind a mask of affability.

I thought of a colleague, an outstanding teacher who lived alone. At lunch I asked him, "How do you live?" He told me his story. Our dysfunctional families of origin were similar in many ways. He had become an alcoholic; AA had saved his life. In his hours outside the university he was mentor to about a dozen recovering alcoholics. I came to understand that I was addicted to control and approval, and that the Twelve Step process could help me to recover, as it has helped people with over 200 other addictions. My colleague agreed to be my mentor on this journey. Before we parted I asked, "How do you think about God?" He replied, "God is reality."

Thus began a rebirth that has continued for over a decade. New experiences of God are the foundation on which my recovery rests. Of the twelve steps, the second says, "Came to believe that a Power greater than ourselves could restore us to sanity." The third says, "Made a decision to turn our will and our lives over to the care of God as we understood him." Here was a challenge: how was I now to understand God? While I was jogging across the fields near home, I thought, "If God is reality, and reality becomes manifest through evolution, God is the Big Process that subsumes all other processes." As I looked at the garden around me I had a vision that affirmed this intuition: The flowers and grasses were like one frame in a time-lapse movie, in which I saw them emerge from the ground, grow, unfurl their leaves and petals. All was rooted and growing in God.

As I worked the twelve steps, I became aware how much about my thinking and behavior I had refused to see for many years. Guilt and sadness accompanied these insights. God as the Big Process was an idea, a comfort to the mind but not the heart. Jogging across the brown grasses of late summer, in distress I prayed, "Lord, make me a vessel of Thy peace." It was so, and I wept in relief and gratitude. Now I knew and felt: I was in God and God in me.

Jay Mittenthal is a member of the Urbana-Champaign Friends Meeting (Illinois). He continues to seek integration between his spiritual and scientific inquiries.

(What Canst Thou Say? May 2003 "Birth and Rebirth")

~ ~ ~ ~ ~ ~ ~ ~ ~ ~ ~ ~ ~

Deciding Not to Pray

Mariellen Gilpin

For a quarter of a century I have been mentally ill. My process of healing from the mental illness has been stepwise. This is a story about one of those steps.

I thought of the hallucinatory pattern as a kind of cycle: First came hallucinations, which shortly intensified in what I called the unseen lover experience; shortly I began conversing with the unseen lover. Once I began hearing voices, it was an extreme effort of will, coupled with heavy medication, to return to reality. My effort for many years was simply to interrupt the cycle. By 1988 I had built up a good track record for interrupting before I heard voices. I was able to cut back the medications.

I began to recognize I needed to stop doing things that brought on the hallucinations in the first place; I needed to take my hand off the trigger. One of the most powerful triggers of hallucinations was the hardest to face: Praying made hallucination almost inevitable. I tried praying less. I tried praying in the morning instead of at bedtime. I tried praying only with a partner. I tried eliminating healing prayer in favor of other kinds of prayer I thought might be safer. My husband labored patiently with me, suggesting that my trigger was like having an allergy to chicken: my task was not to eat less chicken, but to avoid chicken altogether. I resisted; after all, I was trying to build a healthy relationship with God, and prayer was essential to that. Wasn't it?

The crisis came one night when I carefully prayed only "safe" prayers and went to sleep. About an hour later I woke in a state of high rebellion: I wanted to pray for healing, and do so at once. I was still three-quarters asleep, but I prayed for healing. At once the hallucinations began. The unseen lover experience was seconds away. I woke up fully. "Now I've done it," I thought. I turned to God for help.

"God," I prayed, "I'm asking you to help me stop these hallucinations tonight. I admit to you that I am totally responsible for being in this fix. I woke up rebellious and deliberately chose to pray for healing; I was still asleep when I prayed, but the decision was a conscious one. I have to face the fact that 'safe' prayers trigger me to pray for healing, and therefore prayers of any sort trigger hallucination. This is the hardest thing I'll ever do, but I am not going to pray for a whole year, in order to give myself a chance to heal."

Five years. That was the thought that came to me. It was a thought; it didn't come from the part of my brain that I can feel when I am hallucinating. The notion of not praying for five years would never occur to me unaided; it was a completely horrid, impossible concept. I listened, and in the silence I felt rather than thought a complete point of view on my crisis of decision: I had free will; I could do whatever I wanted to do. A five-year commitment not to pray was what God wanted of me. My not praying would please God. What would please God was also taking care of myself. No words had been exchanged; I simply sensed an Attitude. The hallucinations continued.

I believed. "Five years!" I said to God. "One year is impossible to conceive all by itself. Could I make that a one-year commitment that I renew five times? It'd be a lot easier to face." I was bargaining; I admit it. I listened.

Five years. The thought was in my mind again. "I hear you," I prayed. "I'll do it because you asked me. I agree not to pray to you for five years." I paused. This was the last prayer for a long time, and I wanted to say what was in my heart before I hung up the phone. "I want to dedicate every act I do in the next five years to you. Help me pray with my life, since I won't be using words. Every time I choose not to pray is really going to be me saying, 'I love you,' because I couldn't possibly do this just because it's best for me. I'm doing this because you want me to, and I want to please you." The hallucinations stopped, and I slept.

All the next day I struggled to change my mindset. I talked to my husband, who encouraged me. (Actually, he was ecstatic.) I talked to a friend, who offered to lay hands on me and pray. I don't remember a word she said, but I felt better. So it came time for bed, and I realized in my struggle to come to acceptance I had given no thought to what I was going to put in the place of my nighttime prayers. I took a deep breath and rolled over into sleep position. There would be no nighttime prayer substitute; I would simply go to sleep. In that instant, a wave of peace washed over me and saturated my soreness and grief. I knew God was telling me I was doing the right thing, and I slept peacefully through the night.

I wish I could say I kept my word to God faithfully and didn't pray at all for five years. Actually, I made many mistakes, but prayer and hallucination became something that happened monthly rather than nightly. When I no longer had to sort out where reality was every morning, my emotional stamina grew by leaps and bounds. With my doctor's help I was able to make not one, but two medication cuts in the next few months, and within a year eliminated one medication entirely. I learned to pray with my life, and I grew stronger and wiser day by day. I never felt alone; God walked that journey moment by moment by my side.

A year later a Bible study group of very sweet, well-meaning people told me in authoritative tones my spiritual experience was of the devil, and of course I should be praying. I knew I was mentally ill and might well have been misled, and I deeply missed praying. It was a painful time. But I thought about all the gains I had made and remembered Jesus said to the Pharisees, *Every kingdom that is divided against itself goes to ruin.*[19] The devil, if devil there were, would not bring about so much good in my life in order to bring about evil in the end. *You will recognize them by the fruits they bear.*[20] I decided mentally ill or not, I had indeed heard the voice of God—and heard it right the first time.

A week or so later, the group told me not praying was a sin. "But when I pray I hallucinate," I explained. They replied hallucinating was a sin. "Thanks a lot," I thought—as usual, too polite to speak up. "Whether I do what you want or not, I'm sinning. That doesn't leave me a whole lot of choice, does it?" I could not continue to associate with people having beliefs so toxic to me. I believed in the truth of my own experience, and I quit the Bible study.

Within six years, I was able to pray without hallucinating. Why did it take six years instead of five? I certainly don't fault God for not being able to count. A lot of changes had to take place in me before God could restore prayer. But God said five years, not forever, and God was faithful. Glory be to God!

Mariellen Gilpin *is an editor of WCTS. She celebrates the many ways God has helped her deal with mental illness.*

(*What Canst Thou Say?* November 2003 "Spiritual Healing")

~~~~~~~~~~~~~~

Working Around Faith-crushing Experiences

Dalton Roberts

Soon after I became a Christian in my teens, I was playing a yard game at my girlfriend's home. Her mother had been severely ill for months and had wasted down to 70 or 80 pounds. I don't recall the exact diagnosis, but everyone was saying she was terminal. She sent someone out to get me and when I walked into her bedroom, I was shocked at the sight before my eyes. She was just skin and bones. Her eyes were sunk back in her head and she had the color of death.

She said, "Dalton, the Lord just told me if you'd pray for me, I would be healed." I was stunned. I had never prayed in public and had certainly never laid hands on the sick and prayed. But I knelt by her bed and took her hand, or laid my hand on her forehead—I just don't remember—and I stumbled my way through a prayer.

She came up out of the bed and began to praise God. The family all came inside and she told them she was healed because I had prayed for her. If I had a photo of my face at that moment it would reflect complete amazement.

Sure enough, she was healed. She was in church the next Sunday and within a few weeks had gained weight and taken on the glow of a healthy person. Some said I must surely have the gift of healing.

A few years later, I was asked to go and pray for a baby with leukemia. The baby was the first child of a sweet young couple and was clearly the apple of their eyes.

I asked if they believed the child could be healed and they said they did. I took the precious child in my arms and walked the floor, praying with all my heart for a healing. But a couple of weeks later, the child died.

I cannot describe what this did to my spirit. I had felt so certain that the entire room was full of the Spirit of God when I walked the floor with that baby in my arms. I believed the child was healed. I went into a shell. I felt abandoned by God. I felt embarrassed. I wondered if I could ever look those young parents in the eye. How could God allow that baby to die? If an elderly woman could be literally snatched from the jaws of death, why not a beautiful little baby?

I was not helped by watching TV healers. They just popped people on the forehead and they all fell back, then rose to say they were healed. And I couldn't even heal one little case of leukemia. With a crushed faith, I staggered along living a life of joyless routine. I went to church and did all the Christian things, but inside that baby was still dying in my arms.

Sometimes I am saved from despair by my faith but I have been saved more often by my sanity. As great as faith can be, reason can be a more certain savior. Common sense can take us to common denominators that help solve a problem we have scratched all over two big blackboards. I asked myself, "Are all persons receiving prayer healed? Do even those with the gift of healing always heal? Is there any way to guarantee healing to anyone?"

The answer to all my questions was a clear and definite *No*. We need nothing but simple reasoning and observational powers to know these truths.

To give up on God because this Universe is structured a certain way, full of mysteries, unanswered questions and keen disappointments, is to assume God knows less about universe-making than we.

Frankly, I don't understand the presence of pain in a God-created universe, but I do know there have been times when pain has raised my compassion from the dead, and I know there have been times when God has healed my pain, physical and emotional. Yes, it is a mystery, but out of the mystery I have snatched some meaning. I have learned to use pain to expand my soul, to deepen my love, and even to touch people in ways that enable them to find healing.

There are a lot more broken hearts in the world than there are heart attacks. And I know I have been healed of a broken heart by something as simple as a good, long, loving hug from someone brimful of caring love.

If George Fox were here today to say, "You say the church says this about Christ and the Bible says that about Him, but what canst thou say?" I would say, "Brother George, what I can say is that I know Him. I know when I visit the sick, imprisoned or grieving, He goes with me and His presence is sometimes so real I have the witness of those I visit that it helps heal their loneliness, pain and grief. I have the witness of my own spirit that He is real. So real that there are times when He is the most real thing in the world to me, the most meaningful reality in this life I am living."

I cannot say why the elderly lady was healed and the baby died. But the fact that anyone anywhere is healed in body, mind, or spirit proves healing is a reality. And I know most of the healings in my own life have come from being visited, touched, hugged, or just listened to by someone with the love of Jesus Christ in their heart.

God has helped me work around these jagged questions by giving me some answers via meaningful experiences. There are things I don't know, but thank God, there are things I do know. And the sweetest reality is that I am still learning.

Dalton Roberts *is the author of two books, a songwriter, musician, and columnist for the Chattanooga Times Free Press. He enjoys Quaker worship and Unity services.*

(*What Canst Thou Say?* August 2002 "God's Marvelous Workarounds")

~~~~~~~~~~~~~~

Holding Problem People in the Light

Lauren Leach

I am not the person I would have envisioned writing an essay on intercessory prayer. I am not a saint, Quaker or otherwise. Moreover, I confess that I used to view the topic of praying for others with a reluctance characteristic of a child facing a visit to her least-liked great aunt, the one with the bad breath and whiskery kisses and cheek-pinching fingers. Yes, I knew it was the proper thing to do to put the needs of others ahead of my own. But I was needy, and I was hurting, and the pain wasn't getting better, and who was praying for me? In other words, I was the child, who, having endured the visit with the great aunt, demanded of God the Parent, "I've been good—where's my cookie?"

I fell (or was pushed) into the practice of intercessory prayer by the least altruistic of motives. A move halfway across the country had brought me to a small town and a university that seemed provincial, intolerant, bigoted, and dangerously inbred. My students had trouble accepting my East Coast accent and audacious demeanor, and wrote rude comments on my course evaluation forms. My developing romantic relationship with an old college friend had grown confined by the two-and-a-half hour commute between us.

Just when I thought my quality of life had gotten intolerable, a senior colleague at school began targeting me for oblique personal attacks in faculty meetings, culminating in a verbal dressing-down after one meeting for being too involved in research. All my problems, it seemed to me, could be solved by a career change, facilitated by a miraculous job vacancy in the town where my significant other lived. I prayed for this way to open. It did not open.

At this point, angry at God for not listening to me, I called my good friend and spiritual advisor and wailed, "What am I doing wrong? Why isn't God listening to me? What should I be praying for?" He told me I should hold my problems, and the people who were causing me problems, in the Light.

Instantly, the rebellious child within came raging out in full temper tantrum. "Why should I be praying for them? I'm the one who needs help! If I could just get a job in Lawrence, it would solve all my problems! Don't I deserve to have a better job? A good relationship? A life in some town that doesn't have a history of lynching blacks and driving people out of town just because they're different!"

Again, my friend suggested that I pray for all the people and situations that were bothering me, because helping them would at least reduce the pain and frustration they were causing me. And I, as a reluctant but obedient child, began to do so, albeit with a scowl on my face.

My first target of prayer was the colleague who was bullying me. As I held her in the Light every morning, I noticed a gradual change in my perception. I began to see my colleague as a hurt, damaged child who had never grown up and who tried to stuff life's disappointments inside herself by overeating. Indeed, she was who I could have been, would have been, were it not for my years in therapy. I developed a sense of compassion for her.

At the same time, I gained an awareness that she would never be given the impetus to get healthier if I did not challenge her behavior toward me. One day, moved by something (the Light?) I began to use active listening techniques in response to her pot shots, asking her to clarify the messages she was presenting. Although she could neither state what she really meant, nor take responsibility for the damaging statements, she never bullied me again. Gradually I began including other targets, such as the spiritual health of the university and the wider community, in my prayers.

I can say that I feel a sense of relief when I pray for less immediately observable intercessions. Change in a person is easy to spot, but what about change in a community? I will note that, since I have begun praying for the university and community, several things have happened: Faculty hirings are slowly becoming somewhat more diverse. The gay and lesbian student group on campus presented a drag queen show to raise funds for the local Children's Center, which met with amazing success. A colleague of mine recently noted, with some amazement, that she had seen four multiracial couples on campus that week. I feel safer now, living in a town where differences are slowly becoming more acceptable. I don't know that my prayer created any of these new developments, but it certainly couldn't have hurt.

Lauren Leach *is a member of Urbana-Champaign Friends Meeting (Illinois), currently living in Missouri.*

(*What Canst Thou Say?* August 2000 "Called to Intercessory Prayer")

~ ~ ~ ~ ~ ~ ~ ~ ~ ~ ~ ~

As We Forgive Those...

Carol Roth

The stroke had left her with paralysis on her left side and affected her speech. Cancer had spread through her lungs and was now invading her brain. Helpless—terror in her eyes—she looked up at me for help.

I looked down at her as she lay in the hospital bed. The present moment dissolved, and I was a tiny child, trembling as her towering figure charged toward me in a fit of black fury.

Her trembling fingers, the flesh wasting away, reached toward me, and I shrank back, my mind recalling the long, fire-engine-red fingernails which had dug into me, the fingers curling into a fist which had smashed into me again and again. Her mouth twisted as she made an effort to speak to me, but my ears heard only the rasping words of hate and filth which had driven icicles into my frightened young heart.

I was her daughter, now far removed from the horrifying arena of child abuse, but still carrying the scars. The pain she had inflicted was buried deep inside me and I was struggling to forget it. But now, she was dying, begging for the love and attention she had denied me.

We were alone in the hospital room. My siblings had left to prepare dinner for their families. I, too, had been preparing to leave when the nurse told me that my mother's breathing had changed, that perhaps I should stay. Then she left, for no heroic measures were to be taken. Frightened, I had complied. From the window, I could see the headlights of the cars leaving the hospital parking lot in the pelting rain. I wanted to smash out the glass, to scream at my brothers and sisters to return. I didn't want to be alone with her, to be with her when she died.

Once, I had wept for her love, for any sign of maternal attention or affection. Instead, there had been years of verbal and physical abuse and emotional neglect. I had reconciled myself to the fact that she would never love me, and although I continued to see her, to support her in any way that I could, it was merely the dutiful daughter role I was playing. I never dreamed I would have to play it to the end, to her final curtain.

Her breath was coming in tiny gasps. I took a step backward, away from the bed. Her eyes were closed now and I knew I could exit the room, take the elevator, flee from her death. No one would condemn me, not even the nurse, for she knew that in another hospital room across the city my young husband was battling for his life against Hodgkin's disease. Forced to work three jobs to keep a roof over our tiny home for our children, I was exhausted—physically, mentally, and emotionally. The recent deaths of my father and my father-in-law had also drained me spiritually. I was struggling to live in a world grown dark with death. Weary, half-staggering, my heart wrenching, I edged toward her hospital room door.

Her eyes opened and she stared across the room at me. "Oh, God," I screamed in my mind. "Tell me what to do!" She had never loved me. I owed her nothing. "Help me!"

Comfort her. Two words. A direct order, coming from nowhere, yet from everywhere. I froze. *Love her.* A chill went through me. *Love her as you wanted to be loved when you were a child.*

I looked at her. Her eyes were filled with terror. She was afraid of death. Her God was a God of wrath and fury, a vengeful God who punished with fire and hell. Abused as a child herself, she had lived a life of pain and sorrow and had been ill with schizophrenia. This had turned her into a monster, a woman who had fits of fury and uncontrollable hatred. Now she was a tiny, shrunken figure with hysterical fear in her eyes.

Shaking, I took a step toward her, then another. Her eyes pleaded with me and I felt my own face wet with tears. Suddenly, I knew I could not leave and I did what I did with my own daughter when she awakened from a bad dream—I got into the bed.

I clicked off the bright, glaring light in the middle of the room and turned on the soft, overhead night light. Then, gently as I could, I gathered her into my arms and raised her head until it lay on my shoulder. She moaned and I held her tighter, crooning to her, telling her not to be afraid, that I was there, that I would stay with her.

Her slight figure relaxed in my arms. Filled with pity, with compassion, I stroked her hair and whispered into her ear that I loved her, that I had always loved her. She had never allowed me to touch her, ever. Not for her the peanut butter and jelly hands of children. She had had dreams of being a skating queen, until years of poverty and too many children and a husband ill-equipped to handle her mental problems had taken her dreams away. She didn't know how to love—how to give it or receive it—and I knew that now.

Her breathing had changed again. She would take a rasping, struggling breath, then let it out in a long sigh. I knew she was nearing the end of her struggle to live, and I felt so helpless.

Forgive her. And then tell her about me.

Peace filled me. This was something I could do. This was something I needed to do, not only for her, but for myself. The monster had ceased to exist. In my arms was only a woman in pain and fear.

I told her that I forgave her, completely. My tears fell in her hair as I said the words freely, as I assured her of my love and forgiveness.

And then I told her about God, my God, a God of unconditional love, of everlasting love, a God who was in her, in me, in all of us. I spoke to her of the great gift of peace, of love that God had prepared for her. I told her to let go of the fear, to have no fear, for God was Love, waiting to receive her spirit.

I looked into her face. The fear had left. A look of awe, of wonderment, was on her face, and then she smiled at me. It was a smile so beautiful, so filled with love, as innocent, as pure, as my children's smiles. And then, with a sigh as gentle, as quiet as that of a contented child, she died. I continued to hold her, to rock her gently until the nurse returned to the room....

Forgive her. Yes, God, I have.

Carol Roth, *a free-lance writer, was on the editorial team of WCTS in the 1990s.*

(This article was reprinted from *Friendly Woman*, Vol. 8, No. 6, in *What Canst Thou Say?* August 2001 "Forgiving")

~ ~ ~ ~ ~ ~ ~ ~ ~ ~ ~ ~

Living Faithfully

We can be directed, daily, in what we do, the jobs we hold, the very words we say.[21]   —Paul Lacey, 1985

(*What Canst Thou Say?* May 2004 "Guidance")

When God is intimate friend and companion, all of life—painful, ordinary, marvelous—is rich and full of joy. Marti Matthews in "In Defense of the Spiritual Practice of Flossing Teeth" learns driving in traffic can be a chance to practice forgiveness. Judy Lumb ("A Garifuna Healing") is invited to an indigenous ceremony, becomes involved in the needs of the community, and is healed of a longstanding chronic illness.

Our writers think and feel deeply about the problems they encounter and the help they receive. Our spiritual life is a matter of experimentation, of making mistakes and trying to learn from them. It is a voyage of discovery—about ourselves and about God. In "The Ministry of Silent Radiation" Bill Taber works for several years in the spoken ministry, but learns a new calling to silently and secretly nurture the gift of spoken ministry in others. Carolyn Wilbur Treadway in "Do Unto Others" tells of a woman who moves from anger and self-loathing to lovingly supporting an old enemy in his dying.

Spiritual people who are practical seek guidance rather than ecstasies, visions, or voices. They want to know how to deal with life's challenges as God would have them do. Peg Morton, in "A Spirit-led Fast," fasts on the steps of the state capitol to call attention to the cutting of services for people with disabilities. Patricia McBee is unjustly accused during a business meeting, and is helped to focus on the needs of the group rather than her own anger ("The Spirit Took Over"). In "Healing Old Wounds" a friend tells Judith Weir, "Pray for the bastard!" and Judith's own attitude is healed.

The stories in this section are a reminder that God takes us as we are; God teaches each of us the lessons that are especially ours to learn. The wonder is: when we share our experiences the whole world resonates in tune.

~ ~ ~ ~ ~ ~ ~ ~ ~ ~ ~ ~

It is not the great and main work to be found doing, but to be found in doing aright, from the true teachings and the right spirit. It is your proper state to wait daily, not for comforts, not for refreshments (that day is to come afterwards), but for convictions and reproofs of that in you which is contrary to God.

There is a pure seed of life which God hath sown in thee; Oh that it might come through, and come over all that is above it, and contrary to it. And for that end, wait daily to feel it, and to feel thy mind subdued by it, and joined to it. Take heed of looking out in the reasonings of thy mind, but dwell in the feeling sense of life, and then, that will arise in thee more and more, which maketh truly wise, and gives power, and brings into the holy authority and dominion of life.[22] —Isaac Penington (1616–1679)

(*What Canst Thou Say?* August 1998 "Discernment")

~ ~ ~ ~ ~ ~ ~ ~ ~ ~ ~ ~

In Defense of the Spiritual Practice of Flossing Teeth

Marti Matthews

One day I reported joyous news to my spiritual counselor: after perhaps a year of effort, I had finally gotten myself firmly into the habit of flossing my teeth at night. My spiritual director looked quizzical and said, "Great! (pause) But what have you been doing spiritually of late?"

I was taken aback, actually silenced. I had been thinking this was a spiritual accomplishment. We were not connecting here. With effort, I could understand her confusion, and suddenly I saw how very different my spiritual path has become; how far off the traditional path life has led me.

It all has its root in a very severe curvature in my lower back, which doesn't show much but rules my life. It is my Spiritual Guide. It brings me back to earth when my spirit, imagination, or rational mind is tempted to soar too high. It may be my curvature that has also caused me to be abstract—both to think philosophically and to reach out into the Universe for help. My curvature both pushes me beyond the culture and normal life, and then pulls me back into it.

Because of my physical difficulties, I always feel a need for help; even standing on my feet seems a bit much for me. I was shocked that Brother Lawrence had to work to remember God's Presence. I cannot function without that Presence. Perhaps it's because I constantly need the help of this Presence, the Source of my Life, that I find the Presence in everything. Thus, all of life has a spiritual aspect, and the smallest challenge is an opportunity for sacrament. All living is prayer.

I've never understood the logic of the many life-denying philosophies and religions that value life here only as a step to something better somewhere else, or see life as a punishment. Why do we run from the challenge? Why do I even call it a challenge? Life is a wonderful opportunity, and every life is a different opportunity.

Life is a challenge because it can be very difficult. There are tasks that both the world outside us and our own bodies demand—to find food, get out of pain, bond with others, protect ourselves from dangers, resolve conflicts by understanding. These commands are given us to be our universal guide, our boot-camp sergeant, our novice mistress who brings us to our best. We must find work in the community, and in finding our work we actually find our place in creation, our importance, the meaning of our life. In finding what we have to give to the community we also lose our sense of aloneness; we experience the oneness of all, which is a high spiritual experience.

Spiritual challenge and learning are in every small part of life. Why would I need to concoct some spiritual exercise or discipline if I could not even do the disciplines life asks? Like flossing my teeth regularly. Like eating moderately, for the eternal values of both health and beauty. Not denying the goods of the world, and yet using things with awareness and care. There is nothing noble about becoming an unnecessary burden while we save the rest of the world. We are each responsible for ourselves, first of all. The disciplines of healthy, effective, happy living are often more than most people want; perhaps the discipline of religion is an escape from the disciplines we should be facing!

Life is already full of Zen koans. Who has not experienced something they did not understand? Where does this not-understanding take us? It stills the mind and frees us to be again in the present moment with the Presence that breathes us. All Mystery is sacrament. We can write confusing stories for spiritual enlightenment if we want, but we could also just relax into the confusion that's already here and let it carry us into stillness and Presence.

I particularly love the smallest acts of life. Making my bed in the morning feels especially perfect: it's such a simple act that I can wrap my whole being around it and do it perfectly, yet it has such a little goal that I can also be aware of myself while I do it. Bed-making is so gentle. I could almost imagine doing this all day long—making beds, cleaning sinks, scrubbing carpets, experiencing bliss, joy, peace, wholeness as a motel maid. Driving in traffic— a perfectly demanding spiritual task. Forgiveness, non-judgment, letting go of goal-obsessing, going with the unexpected—I'm so grateful for the rigorous daily spiritual exercise of driving in traffic.

I try to meet the silence of my cat and of the house-plants, the emptiness of rational mind, being together without use of words. Again without using thought, I am in relationship with my giant oak and maple. All these presences, my non-rational sisters and brothers, help me feel the unseen Force of which my life is a part, and help me feel the present moment without analysis.

Marti Matthews *is a member of Northside Friends Meeting (Chicago). She has written a book,* Pain: The Challenge and the Gift.

(*What Canst Thou Say?* August 2003 "Celebration and Thanksgiving")

~~~~~~~~~~~~~~

A Spirit-led Fast

Peg Morton

In the wee hours of a July Monday morning, the thought swam into my brain that I could devote the week to a fast and vigil on the steps of Oregon's state capitol in Salem, in support of raising revenue for human services.

I had for many months been involved in the movement to stop the war in Iraq. Meanwhile, Oregon legislators had been enclosed since January inside their marble walls attempting to balance a much-diminished state budget. A small group of mostly disabled people had been trying to raise the attention of the public, and the legislators, to the suffering and instability that was already occurring due to loss of medication and services to thousands of low-income Oregonians. This group approached many of us in the peace movement, asking why we were not involved in their struggle. I am retired from the mental health profession. As a war tax resister, I am very aware of the billions of tax dollars that go for current and past military spending, leaving very little for human needs. Touched by the descriptions of what was happening to disabled people in our state, I began traveling to Salem with the group.

The germ of my idea to fast came from the fact that another woman, Michelle Darr, had fasted, vigiled and camped on the same steps for 56 days and nights during the Iraq war. My heart leapt up and my spirit opened at my idea. There was never any question about a decision. That it might be unsafe to camp out on the steps never occurred to me. I called some Fellowship of Reconciliation friends in Salem that morning to inform them of my plan and ask for assistance. When I arrived two days later, there were Michelle and some of her friends, ready to camp out with me and support me during the following week!

What was happening to me was a spiritual leading. My experience has been that most of the time, but not always, when there was a true spiritual leading, the way opened for it to work out. That was what happened with this fast and vigil. No leading comes out of the blue. For me, this was a part of a long-term leading to make fasting, as a bodily, spiritual and political discipline, an integral part of my life. As an activist with a very full life, this leading represented a pull in a different direction. I couldn't fast and organize!

The leading has unfolded only gradually, while I have waited for my heart and mind to inform me of each next step. I have joined others in day-long fasts around political events, and engaged in a 5-day juice-broth fast on the first anniversary of 9/11. A few years ago, I joined a national two-week fast to close the Army School of the Americas (SOA), and last year I joined some Dominican sisters at the Fort Benning SOA demonstration in a 36-hour water fast.

I began this summer's fast and vigil to raise Oregon state revenue for human services exactly one week following its conception. As I sat there, I was joined and supported by an ongoing stream of people, quite a few of them Friends and/or members of the Salem Fellowship of Reconciliation. They came to sing in the rotunda, to open a House session by singing uninvited, to stand holding signs, to participate in a couple of news conferences and rallies, to make personal visits of friendship, to bring supplies, and to camp out to protect me at night. The nights were incredibly beautiful, with cool, clear air and skies in the intensely hot weather, and glimpses of the new moon.

Many disabled people were among my supporters, taking turns sleeping near me and telling me their stories. One of my new friends was living with AIDS. He was removed from the Oregon Health Plan because, they said, he had not made a payment. It turned out that he had, but the information had not been transferred from the computer to the records. Meanwhile, he was off his medications for two months. Another of my supporters informed me that he too had been removed from the Oregon Health Plan. He lived with Post Traumatic Stress Syndrome, was subject to panic attacks, and feared being around people. He was homeless.

Media coverage for this fast and vigil was extensive and an important part of publicizing an issue that had not been receiving adequate attention and grassroots support. A lobbyist said, "You are lobbying outside while we are lobbying inside." A disabled woman living with mental illness said, "I do not have a voice in there. You are providing a voice for me." Countless people have since told me they held me in their prayers and their thoughts. It became clear to me that we were doing the right thing at the right time, increasing public awareness and involvement. While I was there, I was able to make contact with several legislators. Those personal contacts were important also.

It was exciting to me that two other women decided to fast and vigil on the same steps, consecutively. We were able to have an ongoing presence for three weeks and two days.

When I returned home, the legislature was still in session, struggling. More participants in Eugene joined the grassroots struggle. There was a carefully planned news conference, followed by a line into a cyber-café, where we each could enter letters to our legislators on a computer. And there were many letters to the editor.

The legislators finally voted the budget and went home. Although services were still greatly diminished in Oregon, a fair number of Republicans had joined the Democrats to pass a budget that would restore many services. Taxes were raised to accomplish this. We were informed by some legislators that our presence was helpful in keeping them there, struggling for better results.

Now there is a tax initiative that could well undermine these legislative accomplishments. So the work continues.

Meanwhile, each of us is personally influenced in one way or another by our actions. As I sat there on my juice-broth fast, in the shade of the north side of the building, my body cleansed itself. With expanses of quiet between visitors, my soul was cleaned also, and welcomed the Spirit to flow through me in a way that had never happened to me before. I gave more fullness of attention to those who spoke to me than is usually the case. I thought, "This is the way I am meant to be."

I have thought of legislators, enclosed in their marble buildings, dealing with financial figures, and of corporate executives, inside their glass walls, walled away from the suffering, the real stories of real people.

And now my question is: To what extent am I, and other good people working for justice and peace, separated from the people and groups for whom we try to advocate, separated by the demand of our jobs and families, and in activist time spent in front of computers, on the phone, in meetings, inside the walls of our all-too-homogeneous faith communities? Yes, organizing work is important, but do we, or how can I, find the space to be the way I am, and we are, meant to be—to be more fully human? I am determined to slow down, to leave more space in my life, to spend more time walking and reflecting, meeting and knowing people from diverse backgrounds. Can I do that and not swing back into my beloved old patterns? That is the question.

Peg Morton, *age 73 when this was written, is a devoted member of the Eugene Friends Meeting.*

(What Canst Thou Say? May 2004 "Guidance")

~ ~ ~ ~ ~ ~ ~ ~ ~ ~ ~ ~

The important thing is not to think much but to love much; so do that which best stirs you to love.[23]   —Teresa of Avila (1515–1582)

(What Canst Thou Say? February 2002
"Spiritual Experience and the Outward Life")

~ ~ ~ ~ ~ ~ ~ ~ ~ ~ ~ ~

Tractor Dream

Lynda Schaller

I generally don't pay much attention to my dreams. But over a decade ago, I had a series of dreams about my father. Each dream was a variation on the theme of my dad helping me with his kindly support. In one dream I was floating down a stream which narrowed to an extremely tight space closed in by rock. Dad was a nearby presence; his encouragement helped me negotiate the claustrophobically difficult passage.

Then I dreamed that I was at my parents' house—on the farm where I grew up and where they still live. I stood in the living room looking out at Dad's empty tractor driving itself around and around the house. What, I asked myself the next morning, does a driverless tractor lurching round and round me mean? Though my dad was conspicuously absent from the dream, I knew it was another in my series. I applied the only scrap of dream analysis that I had garnered along the way: a vehicle is the body.

So, the tractor is me. I am lurching around in circles. With no driver. Bingo! Father is not in the driver's seat.

My spiritual background and life at that time included growing up in a Protestant church with an emphasis on a nurturing, caring father-figure God and on living spiritual values as taught by the life of Jesus. Sin, guilt and fear were not given much attention. As a young adult, I kept the values but shed the parts that felt like mythology. I went through agnosticism, atheism, nature and feminist pagan spirituality, and eastern spiritualities, especially Buddhism. By the time of my dream series, I was a seeker ready for a spiritual home. The calling to a spiritual community—a Buddhist one, I thought—was stirring in me.

And then came that dream. My real-life dad does have those positive fatherly qualities of the God of my childhood, and the dream's message became obvious: God needs to be in the driver's seat of my life.

The image of childhood God seated on my dad's red tractor, bumping along a furrow, made me chuckle. And while I had long since laid aside the father-image of God, even the word "God," I found that in thinking about the meaning of my dream, the God of my childhood had tremendous archetypal power for me. While I no longer related to the anthropomorphic and gender-lopsided image, the feeling and direct experience behind the image were juicy and rich—and true. There was something there that I wanted in my life again. With this realization, the dreams stopped.

I didn't know immediately how to integrate and manifest this experience in my life. Eventually I reclaimed the word "God" when I discovered it to be a potent door to my connection with the divine Great Mystery. Over time I moved through other resistances. While some ambivalence remains, that dream metaphor from childhood set my feet on the path that led to my local Friends meeting. Last year I became a member.

I still smile when I think of that tractor. I suspect that sacred silliness is a hallmark of my leadings, that when something pokes me in the ribs and makes me laugh, I should listen up, pay attention. With time, the tractor image has taken on a whimsical animated character, lurching around in circles. While all my phases have been essential to who I have become, I am grateful to have ceased my lurching and circling, and to have settled into my spiritual home and community.

Lynda Schaller is a member of Kickapoo Valley Meeting in rural Wisconsin and lives at Dancing Waters, an intentional community. She cares for a developmentally disabled man who lives with her family.

(*What Canst Thou Say?* May 2004 "Guidance")

~~~~~~~~~~~~~

Only be sure that you act on the message and do not merely listen; for that would be to mislead yourselves. A man who listens to the message but never acts on it is like the one who looks in a mirror at the face nature gave him. He glances at himself and goes away, and at once forgets what he looked like. But the man who looks closely into the perfect law, the law that makes us free, and who lives in its company, does not forget what he hears, but acts upon it; and that is the man who by acting will find happiness. —James 1:22–25

(*What Canst Thou Say?* February 2002
"Spiritual Experience and the Outward Life")

~~~~~~~~~~~~~

The Ministry of Silent Radiation

Bill Taber

Although I had occasionally spoken in Friends meetings since I was seventeen, I was not recorded as a minister by my unprogrammed meeting at Barnesville, Ohio, until I was about thirty-nine. The recording process followed the usual pattern. First, Ministry and Oversight Committee discussed my possible recording without my knowledge and then asked me if I were willing to be recorded, assuming that the monthly meeting agreed to it.

At first I was not sure I should accept, since I was in the process of becoming a released Friend for Ohio Yearly Meeting and did not want it to seem as if I were becoming a paid minister. However my wife and I agreed to feel out (an old Quaker term meaning discernment) the question in a time of silent waiting. To my surprise, both of us sensed that I should accept—not for my sake but because it was important to allow the meeting to recognize the work of God in its midst.

When I said an inward "yes" it was as if a hand were laid on the back of my neck. In my letter allowing the meeting of ministry and oversight to lay this proposal before the monthly meeting, I wrote that if the meeting did see fit to record me, I recognized that I would be accountable to the meeting in the right exercise of my gift.

Having read a number of Quaker journals, I took this matter of being accountable to the meeting quite seriously, although I assumed that being recorded would make little difference other than that I would now attend the meetings of Ministry and Oversight and that I would often be asked to sit on the facing bench.

For whatever reason, the gift increased after I was recorded and I often spoke in my home meeting and the many meetings I visited, as well as in meetings at Olney Friends School. It was not uncommon for one or more people to tell me—often with tears in their eyes—that I had spoken to their condition or that I had answered a question in their mind. Sometimes I worried about how easy it had become for me to speak to people's conditions—I no longer felt the familiar shaking and quaking but had become attuned to the delicate but clear presence of the inward motion out of which living ministry flows.

After several years this ease came to an end, and I found that it became harder and harder to speak in meeting. I often had a strong sense of the message which a given meeting needed to hear—but I found that if I rose to speak, an invisible wall went up between me and the hearers. I knew my words were doing no good at all.

Eventually I remembered reading about this phenomenon in the journal of Ann Branson. She wrote that even if a minister has a true sense of the state of the meeting, it will only add to the minister's confusion to speak without a very clear leading from the Holy Spirit. So I accepted the fact that I was going through a period when—even though I might have an accurate sense of the state of the meeting—I was not to minister with outward words.

Gradually I learned that it was possible to sink much deeper into worship and that when I did sense the need for a message, I could silently pray that the message be spoken by someone else or that it become manifest in the lives of the people present without my words.

Gradually I learned that the most powerful ministry is a wordless radiation of the Love of God. As I began to experience this secret, undramatic, invisible ministry flowing out from me, I realized that my sometimes dramatic gifts in the ministry had depended all along on the secret, silent ministry of a woman here or a man there who never spoke in meeting. With humility I came to understand how their ministry of being deeply present to God and then radiating the Love of Jesus Christ is the most important ministry of all, for it helps everyone in meeting come into a state of living communion and transformation. Words are important, of course—they can be a matter of life and death—but they are only words. What really counts is the powerful transformation of human character which can occur in a meeting deeply gathered into the body of Christ.

Before these insights I had had an intellectual and poetic understanding that the vocal minister is merely an extension of the meeting, of the body of Christ. Now I had experienced how this is so, and I had also experienced how each of us is called to the most powerful ministry—the ministry of secret, silent radiation. When I began to understand all this, I could once again speak in meeting.

Bill Taber *is a member of Stillwater Friends Meeting in Barnesville, Ohio, and a former teacher at Pendle Hill Friends study center.*

(*What Canst Thou Say?* February 1998

"Deepening Worship and Ministry")

~ ~ ~ ~ ~ ~ ~ ~ ~ ~ ~ ~

I or Thou?

Dorothy Neumann

There is a great danger in evaluating our prayers. Whether we are very satisfied or very discouraged with our prayers, the emphasis is on I rather than Thou. For example, I have found a great method for efficacious prayer, or I can never pray well. Both are the opposite of the goal of prayer—to leave self behind to make room for God. Why does God listen, answer and love our prayers? It is the Mystery of Divine Love—unanswerable, but wonderful. How to pray thus becomes how to diminish self-importance so one can give greater attention to God.

Dorothy Neumann *is a member of Urbana-Champaign Friends Meeting (Illinois). The whole day goes better when she prays in the morning.*

(*What Canst Thou Say?* August 2000 "Called to Intercessory Prayer")

~ ~ ~ ~ ~ ~ ~ ~ ~ ~ ~ ~

Stand still in that which shews and discovers; and there doth strength immediately come. And stand still in the light and submit to it, and the other will be hush'd and gone; and then content comes. And when temptations and troubles appear, sink down in that which is pure, and all will be hush'd and fly away.[24]   —George Fox (1624–1691)

(*What Canst Thou Say?* August 1998 "Discernment")

~ ~ ~ ~ ~ ~ ~ ~ ~ ~ ~ ~

Don Quixote and
the Laying on of Hands

Linda Lee

It is four o'clock on Thursday—my time to practice Reiki with Ellen, who has cancer. She stops working. We hug and talk a little. I wash my hands, and when I come back, she is lying on her bed, face up, eyes closed. She has chosen the cello music we both enjoy. Even lying down, her expansive energy is evident. She is ready to receive, and I see her familiar gentle smile.

I sit on a chair, then place my hands on the top of her head. I center into a meditative state. She takes a long breath, sighs. After a while I move my hands to the sides of her head, cover her ears. I am following the ancient Reiki hand positions. I pray, sometimes briefly aloud and always in my mind. "Dear Jesus, let my hands be your hands. Send your healing power to Ellen. Dear God, hold Ellen in your love, be with us now and always."

But words are not enough. I feel the infinite love that is the essence of all existence. I invite that love into full consciousness and presence. If we remove all that blocks divine love, we enter the place of complete healing.

I move my chair to the side and see the fading sun gleam through the wings of an angel at the window. There is snow; the yellow room is bright. On a shelf above is Ellen's collection of statues of Don Quixote, looking toward his impossible dream. I still allow myself the dream of a miracle. My hands are on Ellen's chest and I feel a tingling, buzzing as they get warm, then hot. Almost always I feel a buzzing sensation in my hands, even when there is no unusual amount of heat. Ellen doesn't feel the buzzing, but other energy workers have told me they experience the same thing, so I believe that sensation to be part of the work.

Usually the heat floods in two times during the hour. Sometimes just at the spot Ellen will tell me has been hurting, other times at a place that does not seem to us to be significant. Usually my hands are warm during most of the session, even though the room may be cool. Usually my whole body heats up and I am sweating when the heat comes through. This never happens to me at other times. I am baffled by the whole process. Ellen and I engage in an act of faith; we open ourselves, as much as we are able, to the divine mystery.

For a while Ellen's right leg twitched intensely, to the point of discomfort. I had experienced this myself during meditation and learned it is a release that often happens to people practicing yoga and other meditative disciplines. So I was not concerned about it until Ellen began to be uncomfortable. Her right leg twitched four weeks in a row.

Once we experimented—Ellen's idea. The leg was twitching. I took my hands off. The twitching stopped. I put my hands back. Twitching again. But that was the last week that leg twitched. After a couple of weeks the left leg began doing the same thing, but this time her discomfort was extreme. I consulted with a Quaker healer, John Calvi, whose workshop I had just attended. "Love her like a gentle aunt, not like a passionate lover," he said. So I prayed, "Please send only the amount of energy that is right for her." It was true that I had been holding the attitude of, "Send all the healing you've got, full steam, top speed, flat out, no holds barred." And of course one ought, first of all, to respect where a person is and what is right for them. When I changed my intention, the twitching stopped.

I occasionally use the techniques of Therapeutic Touch used by some nurses. But I don't think technique is necessary. Love is the medicine I invite. Awareness is what I attempt. Healing is my intention and prayer.

Herceptin, a medication, brought a miracle, and love has brought a miracle of another sort. Even though there is a skeptic in me, sometimes I dare to expect more miracles. I put my hands on Ellen's legs. "My bones lit up like a Christmas tree on that last CAT scan," she told me. So I feel the healing love flow into the long leg bones. Ellen lies still, receptive and open.

She has changed so much. Love is flowing constantly in her life now. The old Ellen wouldn't let me get close. The old me would have been afraid to get close, had she invited me. She mixed good doses of anger with her feisty Irish zest and usually dominated our conversations. Now she listens, asks, shares, cares. Laughter still comes freely, but tears also have a place. I feel honored that she accepts and appreciates what I offer. I feel indebted to her; she always gives more than she is given. The love flows and Don Quixote seems to smile when I say, "Love is the miracle."

Yet always, there is this other prayer, this grand, bold request, "Let her be physically as well as spiritually whole." I embrace the paradox and fling this prayer against all that says, "Accept, let my will be God's will;" for I believe in the power of prayer, the influence of intention, the possibility to transcend negativity, the power of love, the possible miracle.

Linda Lee is a member of First Friends Meeting (Indianapolis). She is a former editor of WCTS. Don Quixote was one of Ellen's favorite books.

(*What Canst Thou Say?* August 2000 "Called to Intercessory Prayer")

~ ~ ~ ~ ~ ~ ~ ~ ~ ~ ~ ~ ~

I think I have wasted a great deal of my life waiting to be called to some great mission which would change the world. I think I have been too ready to reject the genuine leadings I have been given as being matters of little consequence. It has taken me a long time to learn that obedience means doing what we are called to do even if it seems pointless or unimportant or even silly.... We need to develop our own unique social witness, in obedience to God. We need to listen to the gentle whispers which will tell us how we can bring our lives into greater harmony with heaven.[25]　—Deborah Haines, 1978

(*What Canst Thou Say?* February 2002
"Spiritual Experience and the Outward Life")

~ ~ ~ ~ ~ ~ ~ ~ ~ ~ ~ ~ ~

The Spirit Took Over

Patricia McBee

I had only been clerk of my meeting for a few months. I was still learning my way, and the meeting was still getting accustomed to me, each clerk having a somewhat different feel. We were discussing a matter which had become contentious over several months, beginning in the previous clerk's tenure. The meeting had divided itself into sides—for and against.

As clerk I suggested those who had concerns about the proposal should speak first. That way, with the concerns out on the table, the proponents could respond to them. Perhaps I would have handled it differently if I had been a more experienced clerk. Or perhaps after the meeting had come to know and trust me as clerk, they would have had greater confidence in my even-handedness. But that is not how it was on that day.

After listening to several people raise their concerns, one of the proponents just couldn't listen to any more of what seemed to him to be relentlessly one-sided. He asked to be recognized and when he spoke he sounded very angry. I observed to him, "Peter, you sound angry." To which he responded in a loud voice, "You're darned right I'm angry. I have never seen such poor and biased clerking." He went on for several more lines and then announced, "I'm not going to stay here for any more of this," and stomped to the door. Apparently on his way to the door he realized he didn't want to miss anything, so as he got to the door he turned and said in an ominous tone, "I'll be sitting out here, and I'll be listening."

After he went out, I turned back to the meeting, and, in a centered and focused way, helped the meeting to continue speaking and listening to one another on the question. We made progress toward unity.

As we moved on to the next item of business and a committee clerk was making a report, I had a moment in which I didn't have to be completely focused on the pulse of the meeting. I discovered I was enraged. I was furious at Peter for having accused me of bias. I found myself resonating to his angry tone and wanting to give him a piece of my mind. I even had thoughts of doing something physically violent. Then I took a breath and refocused on the report that was being presented.

Later, I was amazed at how the Spirit had taken over the clerkship and kept me focused on what the meeting needed after Peter walked out, rather than allowing me to be overwhelmed by my own emotional reaction.

Over the years since then, Peter and I have become good friends. The matter the meeting had been discussing was gradually resolved. Over time I became a more skillful clerk. But I have never been more aware of the Spirit's intervention than I was on that afternoon.

Patricia McBee is a member of Central Philadelphia Friends Meeting. She is on the editorial team for WCTS.

(*What Canst Thou Say?* February 2001
"The Spirit in Meeting for Business")

~~~~~~~~~~~~~

Healing Old Wounds

Judith Weir

My ex-husband and I had been divorced for close to twenty years. I was his first wife and he was just going through his fourth divorce. I was worried about him. He seemed depressed and I thought he might commit suicide, not directly, but perhaps by driving carelessly and getting into a serious accident. I decided to pray for him in a way I had learned some years before in my Al-Anon group. "Pray for the bastard," they'd said. "Pray for him to have what you want for yourself." It had been a powerful prayer the first time I used it, so maybe it would work again.

I prayed for him twice a day from before Thanksgiving until Christmas. The prayer was a simple one. I wished that he would be filled with joy, that

God's love would run through him and out into the world around him, that he would see the beauty of that world more clearly, and that he would deepen his appreciation and love for his neighbors, family, and friends. For the last two weeks I also added wishes that he would learn to walk through his fears and that he might open to receive and follow God's guidance.

The prayer had an effect similar to what I had experienced before. I could feel it changing me. Whether it was affecting my ex, I had no idea. Slowly, all the anger and resentments I felt toward him were dissolving. I had not realized how strong they still were or how deeply I had held them. Now, as my heart grew lighter, I was able to see how destructive these feelings had actually been to me.

A friend and spiritual counselor teased me, saying "You always choose such difficult things to do." He suggested I create a ceremony to mark the end of my period of praying. I decided to have the ceremony at Christmas dinner and invited my ex to join our extended family. No one in the family knew anything about my prayer or about the ceremony I had planned.

Between dinner and dessert I asked everyone to gather in a circle in the living room. I lit a candle in the middle of our circle and said a few words about how this was the darkest time of the year, and that it was good to remember the light we each had inside ourselves and also to reach out to each other with that light. Then I brought out a small wooden mouse that had been part of a cheese board my ex and I had received as a wedding gift more than thirty years before. We had named the mouse Piff, short for epiphany, the day on which we had been married. After explaining this I asked each person there, as a way of sharing our connections and being aware of them, to hold Piff for a short time and then pass him on to the next person in the circle. Piff was passed around the circle, even to the one- and three-year-old grandchildren. After Piff had been around I gave him to my ex, blew out the candle, and we went back in the dining room for dessert. My ex was visibly moved and held back tears as he thanked me profusely.

Several weeks later my middle daughter came to me and said, "Mom, something's changed between you and Dad, and I just want you to know it makes a big difference to me."

Judith Weir *is a member of Twin Cities Friends Meeting (Minnesota) and a writer of poetry and memoir. She has followed a daily meditation practice for more than thirty years.*

(*What Canst Thou Say?* November 2003 "Spiritual Healing")

~ ~ ~ ~ ~ ~ ~ ~ ~ ~ ~ ~ ~

A Garifuna Healing

Judy Lumb

In 1987 I went to Belize for a couple of months—a complete rest—to recover from chronic fatigue syndrome (CFS). I didn't recover, but I developed an interesting life within my relatively severe limitations, centered around desktop publishing from my hammock. Eleven years later I was healed in a Garifuna *dügü* (an indigenous ceremony).

The Garifuna people are an Amerindian-African mix with very strong cultural traditions. I was honored to be invited to a dügü because it is a private, family affair to honor ancestors.

I went to the dügü—in Barranco, the farthest south Belizean village on the coast—assuming that I was an objective outside observer, unrelated to the dügü. By the end of the ten-day dügü I had learned that everyone present is a participant whether they want to be or not. The dügü is a family reunion where both living and dead family members are invited. The ancestral spirits (*ahari*) are invited via the drumming and dancing directed by the traditional priest (*buyei*) and a thanksgiving dinner that is prepared for the ancestors. The ahari appear by spirit possession of their living relatives. They announce themselves and give messages to their living family members, often scolding them.

Initially, although I was invited and everyone did their best to make me feel welcome, I still felt like I was intruding. I tried to blend into the woodwork to be as inconspicuous as possible. The first hint that my attitude was changing was when I sat wondering if my ancestors could hear these drums. I thought especially of my grandmother's great grandmother (six generations back—Grandma Hollenbeck). I had a connection with her because I finished a quilt that she had started around 1900. I also knew that she had a shop and smoked a pipe.

A little while later I was watching the dancing from the northeast corner of the traditional temple (*dabuyaba*) when someone pointed out there was smoke coming in there, so everyone moved out of that corner. The next time I looked at that empty corner, there was an older woman sitting there smoking a pipe. Never have I seen anyone in Belize smoke a pipe! I took that as an answer to my question—indeed Grandma Hollenbeck could hear these drums. The pipe symbol appeared again as Mimi came asking for her pipe, saying she wouldn't eat the thanksgiving dinner until she had smoked her pipe.

I truly became a participant the night that I took spirits home with me. I woke up feeling a cold, blue wind over me, and I heard murmurs coming from the next room. People who have been possessed describe this same cold, blue wind coming at them and then they remember nothing until they wake up again later. I wondered, was a spirit coming to possess me? After lying still for awhile, I got up to see where those murmurs were coming from. I saw my friend Miss Petty sitting in a chair as if she were praying. I don't know how, but I knew that she wasn't real, but the image was there to reassure me. The murmurs were coming from lots of puffs of smoke all around the ceiling and tops of the walls.

When they heard about my spirits, everyone was very concerned, afraid for me. They all asked me what time I left the dabuyaba that night. One is supposed to get smoked by the buyei before leaving, to avoid taking the spirits with you. Of course, I didn't know that and, besides, I didn't think any of that applied to me!

The next day I moved to a different house, and the spirits moved with me. That night when I closed my eyes to sleep, the room opened up into the size of the dabuyaba with murmurs all around the ceiling. I opened my eyes to remind myself I was in a small bedroom, but then when I closed them again, the room opened up again. When I reported this to my friends, they said, "Oh Judy, those spirits are going to molest you. We will have to get rid of them. We'll smoke the house and give you a bath." The smoke was copal and the bath was a bucket with an herbal infusion that I poured over myself. From that time I have not seen the spirits. While my Garifuna friends were very afraid for me, those spirits were a great gift to me, the gift of experience.

Out of that dügü I was led to organize a co-management workshop. In fact I was pulled, kicking and screaming, "I cannot do that!" I could barely walk and had to spend all but about 4 hours each day in bed or hammock—how could I organize a workshop? But each day I was given another piece—the next step toward the indigenous people co-managing with the government the adjacent declared, but not-yet-developed Sarstoon-Temash National Park.

That is another long story, but suffice it to say that I fulfilled an essential initial role, and then appropriate leadership arose from that workshop. Six years later this project is in full swing with significant funding and full participation of the five communities. I follow the progress but have had no real involvement. I now believe my following that leading, however reluctantly, led to my healing two years later.

I had thought that going to a dügü was a once-in-a-lifetime event, but I was invited to a second one, and this time I came prepared to participate. I was invited four ways—in person, via telephone, via email, and from a spirit named "Tony." Tony speaks through his niece, Aura, who speaks only Garifuna and Spanish, but when she is possessed by Tony, he speaks English to me. He told me he was very pleased with my help on another project and that he thought I needed help. He would like to help me, if I would allow it. He told Aura which herbs to give me and then said he would see me in August at the dügü.

I dragged myself to Barranco a week before the dügü was to begin, totally exhausted, and was resting in my hammock. I heard the women were going to clean the dabuyaba in preparation for the dügü that day at 4 pm—Thursday, August 6, 1998. I didn't think I could do anything, but at least I could see people, because I hadn't been out at all since I arrived. I walked in and started collecting soft drink bottles, sweeping, and spreading fresh sand on the dirt floor—an hour and a half later I was still on my feet. For thirteen years I had not been able to stand and talk at the same time!

That night there was a rehearsal. When the drums started, Miss Petty and her daughter Rose said, "Come on, Judy, we're going to dance." I thought, "What, me dance?" I got up and soon got the hang of it. When my legs felt like they were going to collapse, I just said a little prayer, "Just let me get through this one dance" and the feeling went away.

Aura has had a stroke and is paralyzed, but when Tony takes over, he dances—like a man! When I encountered him at the dügü, he said, "Judy! I am dancing!" I said, "So am I, thanks to you!"

I danced throughout the whole dügü, day and night. It was a miracle! When I returned home no one recognized me because my whole countenance had changed so. "Oh, it's you, Judy! You look so different—so light, so bright—what happened?"

It is now five years later and my reprieve continues. I go back to Barranco as often as I can to express my gratitude. My healing has become a part of the dügü legends, and I am asked to tell my story often—to testify.

Judy Lumb is a member of Atlanta Friends Meeting, but lives in Belize, Central America, where she edits, publishes, and writes, mostly about Belize. She is an editor of WCTS.

(*What Canst Thou Say?* November 2003 "Spiritual Healing")

~~~~~~~~~~~~

Prayer is to religion what original research is to science.[26]
—P.T. Forsythe (1848–1921).
(*What Canst Thou Say?* July 1995)

~~~~~~~~~~~~

The Price of Professionalism

Steven Gross

I recently began attending Quaker meeting. On two occasions I have been astounded at what has happened during meeting as I opened myself to the people around me. I noticed experientially for the first time the connection between that which is universal within me and the universal in others. That moment seems to be transforming something deep inside. Now, it seems to be changing how I view my work, which I have always loved and found very fulfilling.

In my work as a public defender, I have chosen professionalism over openness, partly for self-defense and self-preservation—to avoid becoming burned out and dragged down by the pain, despair, anger and hatred that is so apparent in my clients. I also feel it is in my clients' best interest in the long run that I be objective, in order to evaluate their stories and defenses and the case against them as a juror might, without having formed a personal connection with them. By making this choice I deny them experiences that might make the time they spend awaiting trial easier to endure, might even benefit them beyond the trial. But I am first and foremost their legal advisor, and so, though I see a client as pitiful or acknowledge how deprived or abused he or she has been or how limited he is, I have dissociated, remained detached. What price have I paid for this professionalism? What effect has closing myself to connection, refusing to feel the universal that is part of him and me, had on my well-being, my humanity, my spirituality?

Recently, I was forced to re-examine the choice I have made. I was visiting Marilyn in county prison, where she was awaiting trial for stabbing to death her live-in boyfriend. This was the culmination of a ten-year relationship marked by many arguments and physical fights, most of which occurred when they were both drunk. Marilyn was a woman in her mid-forties, an alcoholic for thirty years, who read at a third grade level and hadn't had a job in years. Her two sons were constantly in and out of jail. Her world was depressingly small. She cooked, ate, watched television, and entertained company in her bedroom. Her chief reason for leaving the house was to go drinking at the local speakeasy. She once described a particular speakeasy as being far away, out of the neighborhood. Further questioning revealed it to be a mere three blocks from her house.

On this particular visit I had Marilyn describe her relationship with her deceased boyfriend so I could decide what facts I wanted to elicit at trial. She told me that she loved him, still loved him, and she thought he loved her. Then she stopped and stared off into space and said, "If it wasn't for the alcohol, we could have made it." She rocked her body and nodded her head and said, "Yes, I think we could have made it."

I felt an immediate connection directly from her heart to mine—the universal in her to the universal in me. The feeling was brief but powerful and unforgettable. I know that this connection is always there, always available. What have I missed by not allowing myself to be aware of it, to live it? Can I do my job in a different way? How will my work be different if I allow myself to connect with my clients? How might the universal energy work with my opening up? How will I manage the pain?

Steven Gross *has been a public defender in Philadelphia for twenty-four years, with the last ten in the homicide unit.*

(*What Canst Thou Say?* February 2004 "Open and Tender")

~~~~~~~~~~~~~

Do Unto Others

Carolyn Wilbur Treadway

For the past five years, I have been privileged to be pastoral psychotherapist for "Mary," a hard-working, caring, single woman now in her fifties. Our process together has been profound and also at times profoundly difficult. I have described Mary's journey of rage, angst, self-loathing, suicide attempts, recovery, and transformation previously.[27] This article continues the story of Mary's journey home—home to herself, home to being truly a part of her community and God's world.

Mary had a difficult early life. The middle child of three born to alcoholic, abusive parents, Mary was always the sensitive one. Perhaps she was born an "old soul." She felt everything keenly, but had no outlet for her feelings, and very little support, guidance, or nurture. She grew up tough, reflecting the chaotic and sometimes brutal environment all around her. Her inherent gentleness and compassion were not called forth, yet remained inside her as vulnerability and incredible pain.

Again and again over her lifetime, her family and the world mistreated her and destroyed her hope and her ability to trust. Her anger increased and her sense of her own worth remained in the cellar. An incident of intense rage toward her extended family during a holiday dinner, in which Mary splattered the turkey all over the festive table, frightened her (and her family) and precipitated her entry into therapy with me.

Mary had been in therapy many times over the years. But from the start, this time was different. Perhaps this time it was God's timing. From the start, we somehow connected and wrestled deeply with the myriad issues of her present, past, and future, especially with her pattern of self-abusive acting out in order to get attention, the attention fading away as the crisis diminished, and her rage only increasing.

A dramatic incident occurred several years into therapy when, acting out of her old self-destructive pattern, Mary attempted suicide in my office by swallowing a bottle full of pills in one giant gulp. I accompanied Mary to the emergency room for stomach pumping and her admission to psychiatric intensive care.

While in the emergency room, Mary told me she would not leave the hospital alive; she would definitely find some way to kill herself while there, and I most certainly would not see her alive again. I believed her. She was cold, unreachable, and determined—and she had wanted to die for many years. My instantaneous response to her announcement was to cry. A woman I cared deeply about was saying goodbye, albeit cruelly, and I was taking her seriously, and grieving. I knew the limits of my ability to help her, and we were past them.

My tears continued to flow during much of the time we remained in the emergency room, as I continued advocating for her life and for God to help her make a different choice. They flowed as I told her I definitely did not want her to die at her own hand, but if she was going to die I was not going to abandon her, I was going to love her and believe in her right up to the very end.

As it turned out, my spontaneous tears helped to save Mary's life. They were transformative for her. She could not believe anyone cared enough about her to cry over her at all. Nobody ever had. Nobody ever would. Nor would anybody ever really care about her. But now, somebody did. My tears reached her at a level my words could not. I cared. Mary had made a connection, after all. She did matter to someone, to me. These slowly dawning realizations changed Mary's view of herself and her world. Gradually, they changed her life. Many times since then, Mary has talked of this time in the emergency room and of my tears which started to change everything for her. To this day, I believe those tears were the expression of God's love for Mary. I was only the channel, the vessel.

A couple years passed, during which Mary grew calmer, stronger, clearer, and happier. Her brother-in-law—one of the people who had earned her rage at that holiday dinner—became more and more ill with complications from diabetes. As John declined, Mary became increasingly appreciative of and loving toward him. Instead of being frequently angry and frustrated with him—often for very good reason—she became much more accepting of him. John was unaware, but Mary was not. She saw him struggling with his own life journey, just as she had struggled so long with her own. Her compassion for him grew and grew.

In a wondrous way for one who had recently devalued her own life so much, she longed to help John live his remaining life to the fullest. Beyond this, Mary wanted to help John with his dying. She wanted to be with him, loving and believing in him right up until the very end. Very deliberately she sought to "do unto him" as she had experienced me "doing unto her" in the emergency room. She remembered vividly, and used her experience—in a marvelous way—toward the healing of John, even in his dying.

Mary had a special talk with John; she advocated for his life and for him to take better care of himself. They expressed appreciation and caring for each other, and she told him she would be with him as he became sicker. Only a few days later, John peacefully died in his sleep. Mary was very upset she had not been with him at the time of his passing. I thought she really was with him in spirit, and that he knew she really was present for him all the way to the very end.

Mary gave the eulogy at John's funeral. She talked of missing her fishing buddy, of his love of his family, and of his incredible persistence in getting through many hard times. She learned from his life, and he from hers, for with her heart and her actions in his last days, she lived out doing unto him as she had always wished he (and others) would do unto her. This, to me, is another marvelous workaround from God.

Carolyn Wilbur Treadway *is a pastoral counselor and family therapist in Normal, Illinois. A lifelong Quaker, her spiritual practice includes frequent trips into nature with her camera and an open heart.*

(*What Canst Thou Say?* August 2002 "God's Marvelous Workarounds")

~ ~ ~ ~ ~ ~ ~ ~ ~ ~ ~ ~ ~

One step taken in surrender is worth more than an ocean journey without it.[28]   —Meister Eckhart (1260–1327)

(*What Canst Thou Say?* August 2002 "God's Marvelous Workarounds")

~ ~ ~ ~ ~ ~ ~ ~ ~ ~ ~ ~ ~

Contemplative's Prayer

Heidi Blocher

Dearest, beloved God
the more you want me for yourself,
the more you want to share me with the world.

Let me and my life and my destiny
rest in your hands.
Let me obey and go from that rest
to your beloved world, carrying
rest within me, the seed
for which the world yearns, seed
from which the crop will spring
that will still its hunger.

Dear God, as I walk along
in the barren field,
do not take your hand from under me
nor from around me
nor above me.

Mercifully keep me in the darkness
of your rest, letting your Light
shine from it, invisible to my eyes.

Sweet Lord, keep me gathered
to you, in every step.
Triumph, my Lord, as you live in me,
secretive Victor.

Let me entrust myself
fully to your mysterious
workings as I walk, seeking nothing
but your rest, your clinging, your simple and dark
guidance.

Heidi Blocher *is a member of Sandwich Friends Meeting (Massachusetts).*
(*What Canst Thou Say?* April 1996)

The Nature of Holy Obedience

Thomas Kelly

Some come to holy obedience through the gateway of profound mystical experience. It is an overwhelming experience to fall into the hands of the living God, to be invaded into the depths of one's being by His presence, to be without warning, wholly uprooted from all earth-born securities and assurances, and to be blown by a tempest of unbelievable power which leaves one's old, proud self utterly, utterly defenseless.... Dare one lift one's eyes and look? Nay, whither can one look and not see Him? For field and stream and teeming streets are full of Him. Yet as Moses knew, no one can look on God and live—live as his old self. Death comes, blessed death, death of one's alienating will....

One emerges from such soul-shaking, Love-invaded times into the more normal state of consciousness. But one knows ever after that the Eternal Lover of the world, the Hound of Heaven, is utterly, utterly real and that life must henceforth be forever determined by that Real. Like Saint Augustine one asks not for greater certainty of God but only for more steadfastness in Him....

Do not mistake me. Our interest just now is in the life of complete obedience to God, not in amazing revelations of His glory graciously granted only to some.... States of consciousness are fluctuating. The vision fades. But holy and listening and alert obedience remain, as the core and kernel of a God-intoxicated life, as the abiding pattern of sober, workaday living.

Once having the vision, the second step to holy obedience is this: Begin where you are. Live this present moment, this present hour... in utter, utter submission and openness to Him.

And the third step in holy obedience... is this: If you slip and tumble and forget God for an hour, and assert your old proud self, and rely upon your own clever wisdom, don't spend too much time in anguished regrets and self-accusations but begin again, just where you are.

Yet a fourth consideration in holy obedience is this: Don't grit your teeth and clench your fists and say, "I will, I will!" Relax. Take hands off. Submit yourself to God. Learn to live in the passive voice—a hard saying for Americans—and let life be willed through you.[29]

—*Thomas Kelly (1893–1941)*

(*What Canst Thou Say?* February 2002
"Spiritual Experience and the Outward Life")

Reflections on Living Reverently

Marlou Carlson

I have learned something valuable about the rhythm of activity and reflection in my life and how work needs to be centered. It has been more than two years since I retired from my day job. It was an early retirement, taken with much gratitude for many fulfilling years of teaching elementary school, and with the deliberate intention of having more time for the volunteer work that I was already doing among Friends. For several years before my retirement, I had felt moved to work in religious education. Without much introspection, I had agreed to serve on the Religious Education committees of my monthly meeting, yearly meeting, and Friends General Conference (FGC). Through the FGC committee, I became involved in the new Traveling Ministries Program.

As a retiree, I hoped to do all this work more thoroughly and perhaps even add a dimension or two. I was expecting time to open before me like an expanse of blue prairie sky. It didn't. I was expecting tasks to be like play because I was so eagerly anticipating them. They weren't.

Among the first lessons presented in my new life was the contrast between work required by employment and work undertaken by choice. In the former, decisions are made according to convention or by someone else. An individual approach may be taken toward how certain tasks are accomplished, and the results may take on a distinctive flair. Still, the individual has not chosen that task nor discerned whether it is fitting.

Work undertaken by choice needs a different quality of discernment and careful centering in God. As the days went by, I noticed I was experiencing my Quaker volunteer work much the way I had experienced the unchosen tasks of my public school work. Somehow I hadn't discerned whether I was called to it and nor held it up in prayer.

I still yearned for the time to pursue interests, engage in favorite pastimes, and heed artistic whims. As I worked, God wasn't present in my heart to the extent I had anticipated. I was surprised. I expected when the pressure of the secular schedule was removed there would be a great sense of relief and joy, and the presence of God would automatically flood in to infuse my work.

A longing for joy in the presence of God very soon led to establishing a spiritual practice as the anchor of each day. Every morning came to include a time of reading both inspirational pieces and scripture followed by prayer and worship. The blessing was that now there was time unscheduled by the secular world in which to enjoy this practice.

It was something of a shock to discover that all sorts of things needed discernment: which tasks to continue, which to lay down, which to do now, which to do later, and which new tasks to consider. It was not just the important tasks of clerking the First Day School committee, or writing my piece for the book for Quaker parents, that needed discernment and prayer. It was everything. Dusting, dishwashing, and weeding all needed discernment and prayer. All the mundane things of life needed to be held in prayer if I wanted to experience the presence of God in all those things. If I wanted to experience the joy of God's presence during the committee meeting, I needed to invite God's presence while I packed the suitcase. If I wanted God's presence during the time set aside for writing, I needed to invite it while I dusted the desk and sharpened the pencils.

The next lesson was about the number of activities that could be sustained in the reverent life. As I began consistently to hold each undertaking in prayer, I noticed that when it was set aside for the day or completed, I would sink into quiet and reflection, giving thanks. Sometimes, the number of minutes needed for this period of reflection was large. I noticed that God spoke in these quiet times and that I wanted to listen attentively. These became times of savoring the enjoyment of work or of satisfaction in a job well done. A rhythm of reading, prayer and worship followed by work, then reflection and thanksgiving, blossomed in my daily life.

It seemed if one allowed this rhythm to flow, enjoyment and awareness of God's presence increased. The light in the shiny glass, the warmth and softness of the dry towel, the beauty of the polished surface, the fragrance of a plant, the regular angles of a stack of stamped envelopes, brought that deep inner joy, God's blessed presence. During these quiet times my attention would eventually be called to the question of what should come next. With prayer, I would be able to discern the next step or task. More and more the work became God's.

More and more I noticed that I was too busy. There were simply too many tasks to give time to this naturally developing rhythm. If I did all the tasks on the list, I wouldn't be able to yield to the rhythm. The rhythm was God-given. I longed to comply.

How was it that I had taken on all these many tasks? Pondering, I saw that I had considered myself unworthy unless I was in service to others. If I was not doing good works, I was nobody. For years I had been committing the great sin of not believing I was a worthy soul, a true child of God, by just being. When I saw a need, I plunged right in to fill it, correct it, save it, or do it right. The question, "Is this my task?" had not been examined. Without thinking, I had planned each day with one task after another. I had joined the hectic society of frantic over-doers. Even in retirement I was overwhelmed and uncentered.

Over the years I have delighted in sharing responsibilities with others whose developing gifts I am encouraging. The discernment and calling forth of the gifts of others are peculiar Quaker skills that I treasure and am gratefully learning more about through the experience of the School of the Spirit. Yet I perceive that upholding another is also a kind of work. Being a presence while another is growing in the Spirit requires a level of energy that I have come to appreciate anew.

In some cases sharing the responsibility is harder and requires more thought and prayer than doing the particular task oneself. Nurturing another is work, inspired by God, demanding prayer, centeredness, and time for reflection and thanksgiving. The lesson seems to be that in discerning whether to take on certain work, thought needs to be given to the care of others.

One does not do Quaker volunteer work in a vacuum. A considerable amount of the work is done in committee meetings or in pairs. Carrying out the will of God requires loving attention to the others involved in that work. Everyone needs to be encouraged to listen to the still small voice. Another part of this lesson is that the aspect of nurturing others increases the magnitude of spiritual energy in the work. The amount of attention needed for any given task, then, is increased, however lovingly, by the need to be a nurturing part of the community. Again I felt the longing to yield to the rhythm. I longed to be always centered in God, to embody a deeper level of respect for other children of God and for God's work, to live in an attitude of reverence.

This longing leads to less work, more carefully chosen, with enough time left for centering every aspect and for worship, prayer, reflection, and thanksgiving. I ache for simpler tasks, done more reverently, for the glory of God. More listening and less work seem imperative. Gently laying aside some of my work seems right. The more work laid aside, the clearer is the call to do so.

In *Wisdom Distilled from the Daily: Living the Rule of St. Benedict Today*, Joan Chittister describes treating everything as though "they were the vessels of the altar." To hold life in loving hands is a call that compels contemplation. Yesterday I set my word processor to printing in tiny, pretty letters on a scrap of bright yellow card stock, the prayer of Niklaus von Flue, Swiss saint. It just fits in my hand.

My Lord and my God, take all from me that hinders me on my way to Thee.
My Lord and my God, give all to me that furthers me on my way to Thee.
My Lord and my God, take me from me and give me wholly to Thee.

Marlou Carlson *is a member of Duneland Friends Meeting in Valparaiso, Indiana. She has served FGC Traveling Ministries Program.*

(*What Canst Thou Say?* May 2001 "Solitude")

In Celebration

I was at the plow… and suddenly I heard a voice saying to me, "Get thee out from thy kindred and from thy father's house." And I had a promise given with it, whereupon I did exceedingly rejoice that I had heard the voice of that God which I had professed from a child, but had never known him…. And when I came home I gave up my estate, cast out my money; but not being obedient in going forth, the wrath of God was upon me, so that I was a wonder to all and none thought I should have lived. But after I was made willing, I began to make some preparation…. Shortly afterwards going a gate-ward with a friend from my own house, having an old suit, not having any money, having neither taken leave of wife and children, nor thinking then of any journey, I was com-manded to go into the west, not knowing whither I should go, nor what I was to do there. But when I had been there a little while, I had given me what I was to declare. And ever since I have remained not knowing today what I was to do tomorrow…. [The promise was] that God would be with me, which promise I find made good every day.[30] —James Nayler (1616–1660)

(*What Canst Thou Say?* November 2000 "Visions and Voices")

~~~~~~~~~~~~~

When God is intimate friend and companion, problems persist but life has meaning and purpose and joy. Even chronic illness becomes joy when God has called us. Terri Mittenthal loses all her roles in life when she develops chronic fatigue syndrome, but finds she is still a child of God. In "Joy, Intention, Prayer, and Gratitude" Christine O'Brien has lupus, and takes joy in a continuing sense of God's presence.

Living and working in the presence of God brings awe, grace and gratitude. In "The Healing Harp" Sabrina Sigal Falls receives the gift of playing the Celtic harp at the bedside of the dying when she moves beyond her feelings of limitation, doubt and concern. Carolyn Smith Treadway ("Liking What I Have to Do") learns it's not doing what she likes to do, but liking what she has to do, that makes life blessed.

God has special work for some of God's special friends. Marcelle Martin ("A Request for Release") is given a ministry among Friends—and no steady income. Kathryn Gordon, who struggles to make ends meet, is moved by God to give money for Marcelle's ministry—before she has the money to give ("The Four Thousand Dollars"). Both women must step out in faith. In "Belize Park: From Dream to Reality" Judy Lumb is given the mission of helping her Garifuna and Kekchi friends arrange to co-manage a national park. She was chosen not because she could do the work—she spent most of her days in a hammock because of chronic fatigue syndrome—but because she was tendered to God's will and knew who to call.

In "A Time of Celebration" the mystery at the core of the universe turns out to be beneficent when Mariellen Gilpin prepares to weep over the death of her favorite uncle, but finds God is with her always. In "Stretch out Your Hands" Maurine Pyle is willing to bear a message to a woman she doesn't know—and the message is a stunningly specific blessing. Jennifer Elam in "Thank You, God, for All of It" learns God can take any mistake she makes and turn it into good. And Carol Roth decides in "Opting to Live" she will live in attention, in awareness, in appreciation that she is just as human as she is spiritual, and takes joy in the process. May we all live in the spirit of joy these authors share.

~ ~ ~ ~ ~ ~ ~ ~ ~ ~ ~ ~

Joy, Intention, Prayer, and Gratitude

Christine O'Brien

I got Lupus and lots of its entanglements when I was twenty-five. The doctor told my parents and me that I would probably die within the year. I am fifty-three now and have been healed many, many times but not always in the expected way.

I am very sick right now, and sometimes in the middle of the night when I am in pain and can't sleep, I find my mind wandering ferociously in darkness. I know this darkness well, and yet I am always surprised by it. It carries me far from my usual equanimity into a terrible land of anger and dis-ease. Fortunately, this frustration doesn't last long with me. In a few days or weeks of illness I relax into the darkness and let it enfold me. I feel I am a boat floating high above my anchor, drifting far out one way and another with the wind and water, but anchored always. I was resting, again, in this image last night for hours and for the first time asked myself, "What is it I am anchored to?" Strangely, I am anchored and comforted by the surety of my life's change within the continuing change of the earth, of which I am a small, yet for me, important process. I am a process in motion from birth to death. I am like the grass, springing up at times and then laid low.

The long night is the hardest time for me. If I need something with more energy to think about, I think about colors. I think about the vivid colors that I love and I combine them with each other in ways that make me feel joy. It is a very simple practice with no real outcome except for joy. Thinking and thinking of colors is, for me, a delight.

In the daytime I move slowly from task to task if I am able. I like to work, so I keep on. I give up all things that do not feel healing to me. I simplify, with no sense of loss. Life stripped bare shows its beauty.

It is my intention to have a life separate from my illness, or in spite of it. I feel such joy that, when I am well enough, I can do work that I love. For twenty-four years, I clerked our Meeting, and continue to play a vital role in it. I organize peace festivals, do graphics for this or that good cause, and I paint. I give workshops on lots of things that are important to me. For the thirty-second year, I will again organize Circus McGurkis the People's Fair. I try to make my life a prayer—a prayer for healed societies and families and spirits.

When I'm getting too weird on my medications or I'm too sick or tired to work, I go to bed and look at the leaves and sky outside my window. I stare intently at them and then I close my eyes and rest, turning inward toward Spirit, cradled in the everlasting arms. Even if this is all I can do, it is all I need to do. To hold and be held.

Gratitude is essential. Gratitude lifts my heart and helps me see the beautiful light shining above the darkness. Each of us is a beloved child of God. It is true parts of me are ill, but all of me is held by Spirit. It is hard to remember this if I am not whole, so I work on feeling whole. I use leaves and sky a lot. I am extremely grateful that we have sky-clad leaves and an atmosphere with wandering clouds.

The leaves, besides being beautiful, remind me of the cycle of life and death. Every spring, here in Florida the leaves fall off my trees, pushed off by the baby leaves, and for two or three weeks I see the naked sky. It shows me again that everything has its season, and I am glad to share this journey with the leaves. The clouds remind me that you just never know. There are surprises at every turn and almost anything is possible. I am comforted that nature will always work no matter what we do.

While it is true that I am "better living through chemistry" and drugs keep me alive, I believe most anything can heal you on some level. Joy, intention, prayer and gratitude are the most powerful healing agents.

Most of my life I have handled my illness on my own. Recently I have learned to accept help from my beloved and have become brave enough to let my Meeting and my friends know when I am ill. I know they hold me in the Light every day, and I feel held up and supported always. I don't go out much but I live very happily, and am highly entertained within my house and garden. I have fabulous books on many subjects and fascinating paintings and pottery, exotic seedpods and tiny animal skulls from the garden. I can wander around my home and feel as though I have visited an amazing and meaningful museum.

I have been blessed in my life, since childhood, with a continuing sense of the Presence. When I spin away from it in illness of mind or body, I must turn back to it again in the depths of my spirit. This underlying gift, always within my reach, if I am true enough, has blessed my life in every aspect. I feel certain that the Presence within has an incredible healing power. I don't know if it heals my body, though certainly the calm stillness in my center must help. I do know I am healed in spirit, as I turn toward the divine breathing.

My family gathered here last weekend for a reunion. The best part was when my sisters and I were singing the old hymns, holding the resonating harmonies a long, long time, really sinking into all the old chords. Feeling those chords vibrate, being in them, the voices blending as they always have, in that moment I was absolutely healed. In that moment, the wings of the Beautiful enfolded us and changed all to Light.

Christine O'Brien *recently retired from being clerk of St. Petersburg Friends Meeting (Florida) for 24 years. She has been an activist since she was a teenager.*

(*What Canst Thou Say?* November 2003 "Spiritual Healing")

~ ~ ~ ~ ~ ~ ~ ~ ~ ~ ~ ~ ~

A Child of God

Terri Mittenthal

Eleven years ago chronic fatigue syndrome came barreling out of the blue into my orderly world and mugged me. It knocked me down and robbed me. It took from me my ability to make a living, my ability to drive my teenage children everywhere they needed to go, my ability to put food on the table, to keep order in my home, to have a thoughtful conversation with my husband, to walk, to sit unassisted. I thought it had robbed me of myself. Who was I? Who was left? I had always identified myself with the roles I played. I never said, "I work in the nursing field." I said, "I am a nurse." Now, I thought, I had no roles and therefore no identity.

Through the blessing of time—time to think, time to pray, time to be alone with myself—time I had not chosen to take before it was thrust upon me—I have come to realize that I am not my work. I am not the tasks I accomplish. I am not even what I think. None of these things is the essence of me. I am something that can never be taken, no matter what hardship might befall me, no matter how strong the mugger. I am a child of God. I rest in this in the hardest times and I rejoice in it in the best. It does not change. We are all children of the Divine.

Terri Mittenthal is a member of the Urbana-Champaign Friends Meeting (Illinois). "My spiritual practice includes daily (mostly) meditation, and attention to the presence of God in all things. Another blessing my brokenness has given me is time to paint. I'm always challenged to paint the Presence in the ordinary things I see around me or within me."

(*What Canst Thou Say?* August 2000
"Wholeness in the Midst of Brokenness")

~ ~ ~ ~ ~ ~ ~ ~ ~ ~ ~ ~ ~

The Healing Harp

Sabrina Sigal Falls

My Celtic harp is truly an instrument: the instrument of God's love and care for me, and the instrument of my ministry to others in gratitude and service to God. Both the harp itself, and the way I play it, came to me as a serendipitous gift, which I believe is of the Holy Spirit. Those who have had this kind of experience know there is no rational explanation for such a gift, no way it was earned or deserved or even requested.

I never asked God for a harp. In fact, before the notion of playing the harp was gently nudged into my heart and mind one First Day in meeting for worship, I had not taken much notice of harps. I had never even come near one! I had, however, taken much notice of traditional Celtic music, which I had been enthusiastically listening to for about ten years by this time (1985). Although I enjoyed the harp as one of the traditional Celtic instruments, my favorites were the uillean pipes, fiddles, and flutes—not the harps!

My first message from the Spirit came when I returned from an intense two-week visit with family, the first week at my parents' home in Grand Rapids, Michigan, and the second in Toronto, Canada. My sister and my husband flew out to Grand Rapids with me to be with my father in the last week of his life after seven months of colon cancer. With the blessed help of hospice staff and volunteers, and our mother's devoted care, he was able to die at home. So we shared those final hours with my dad and were present at his last breath.

Then came the funeral in Grand Rapids and the burial in Toronto, where my father had been born and raised. We buried him in the cemetery plot shared by generations of relatives, including his parents. According to Jewish custom (Judaism is my spiritual foundation), we "sat shiva"—mourned together for seven days in my uncle's house with friends and family in and out and nightly worship services in the living room. My husband had returned home several days earlier than I, so when I got back to Philadelphia, where we were living at the time, I came home to an empty apartment in the middle of the afternoon. I proceeded to unpack and avoided feeling.

To break the boredom and silence, I put on one of my Celtic music records. Suddenly, I had to stop what I was doing and just sit and let the music float around me. It surrounded and filled me with its wondrous harmonies and rhythms and, rather than the deep sorrow and weariness I had been feeling for so long, I actually felt joy and peace. How I loved this music! I had always loved traditional Celtic music, but suddenly I realized that its effect on me may be more significant than simply a matter of musical taste. The message spoken within me said, *this music really affects you powerfully. Pay attention.*

Shortly thereafter, I was given that beautiful, unexpected gift during meeting for worship when the image of the Irish harp came into my mind, together with the message: *You could play this.*

"Right. Uh, I don't think so," was my initial reaction. The whole notion struck me as impossible. A person in her late twenties simply doesn't take up a new instrument that she knows nothing about or where to get and can't even afford! I probably would not have taken it any further, except that, in the next few days, whenever the thought and image floated back to me, I felt a sense of lightness and happiness I could not ignore. For much of the past year, I had been walking around with a dark cloud hovering over me and a pained, hollow heart. All of which had no helpful explanation besides the obvious fact of my father's illness and death, but which certainly went deeper than that. It was the kind of depression, with its hopelessness and sadness, which debilitated me inwardly while I functioned fairly normally outwardly. Nobody but I knew the depth of my inward suffering. But the idea of playing the harp filled me with a joy that I had not felt in a long time.

As the *pay attention* message played back to me, I knew God was touching me and that I had to have faith and say "Yes." Instantly, that heavy cloud was lifted, miraculously, as if this harp had wings! I had experienced God's healing, but only in relationship. It would not have happened, I don't think, without my participation, my willingness to accept the gift in spite of my limitations and doubts and concerns and questions. Much to my delight, many of the obstacles I had anticipated were removed. Doors opened, and in not too long a time, I was able to obtain a harp and a teacher and start on my way to living out the leading. By now I recognized it as being of the Spirit.

The other gift God gave me was that of playing the music by ear. At my first harp lesson, I expected to learn the music from musical notation, that is, reading music just as I had done in my background of playing piano and singing in choirs. But much to my surprise—and dismay—this was not to be. My teacher, a traditional Celtic harper, said she would play the tune, I would watch and listen, and then I would play it.

But I don't play by ear! I don't do this. I need to read the music. No, dear, she said. This is traditional music. It's not written down; it's passed on from person to person. You learn the tune and then you make it your own.

I had no choice, and that was the best gift I could have received! The great spiritual growth in this for me was that I was thrust into using the much-neglected right side of my brain. I was always—and still am—a left brain person. I needed balance. Although I had assumed that I was not capable of playing by ear, I quickly discovered otherwise; but don't ask me how it happened or where it comes from or why it isn't hard for me at all. Or, do ask—because the answer is good: it comes from the Holy Spirit, where else? This is not my talent or ability, but God's kindness to me in playing beautiful music through me. Both my harp and I are instruments for God's word communicated in music.

Playing music on the harp is, for me, an act of co-creation with my Creator. Whenever I take a familiar tune and work up an arrangement for it, it becomes a new creation. I do not play only Celtic music, but also hymns, spirituals, some contemporary popular things, some Jewish melodies, lullabies, folk songs, and even the "Pachelbel Canon in D"—I did use some musical notation to get started on that one! It is often a worshipful experience for me, because the music comes straight from my heart. Since I don't depend or rely on notation, the music must flow from a deep place within myself. I must dig deep inside my soul, explore my feelings, and release them in the way I play the music. Although I do practice diligently in order to perfect my skill, I believe that the impact my music has on people has much more to do with allowing God's Spirit to flow through me and my harp than on technical expertise.

Since that first experience of divine healing, I have had more bouts with depression and anxiety. Although I have not again enjoyed that same sudden lifting of sadness or emotional turmoil, the harp has indeed been a saving instrument for me during some of my hardest times. Most recently, I was in the midst of a very trying time when I realized I had the opportunity to enroll in a program that would train me to be a music practitioner—to use the harp in a ministry of healing at the bedside of the sick and dying. This had been a dream of mine ever since the beginning of my beautiful harp journey. Following this leading—despite more obstacles, hardships, and financial sacrifices—once again gave me a sense of purpose to live and thrive, and I see that it has made a difference in the lives of others.

Now I am a certified music practitioner and play for the sick and dying for healing or transition. Playing at the bedside, I have had some of the most powerful spiritual experiences of my life. To accompany a soul as it floats from this life to the next; to enable an agitated AIDS patient to lie down and rest; to hear a woman with Alzheimer's sing to familiar strains; to ease the headache of a man with a brain tumor; to help a young cancer patient visualize her honeymoon on a tropical island—these blessings and more cause my soul to rejoice in the love, kindness, and constant faithfulness of God!

Sabrina Sigal Falls *is a recorded Friends minister and harpist living in Indianapolis, Indiana, where she attends First Friends Meeting. Her first CD is* Healing River.

(*What Canst Thou Say?* May 2002 "Arts and the Spirit")

~ ~ ~ ~ ~ ~ ~ ~ ~ ~ ~ ~

Love

Mike Resman

These eyes have never seen You
    my love,
and I know I never shall.

I am content to contemplate
the nearest glimpse of You;

The reflection of a butter cup—
dew drop's gleam—
green of a hillside painted with a forest.

I will look for You with my heart,
where I see You shining
through a million suns.

Nor will this skin be touched.

But my soul,
what You've done.

I'm immersed in a Love bigger than time—
past space—
my every particle
infused, permeated, saturated
love
comfort
peace
grace

You.

Mike Resman *is a member of Rochester Friends Meeting (Minnesota).*
(*What Canst Thou Say?* May 1995)

A Request for Release

Marcelle Martin

Just before the conference on Mysticism Among Friends Today at Pendle Hill in October 1996, I had an experience of a great force or transforming power that God was sending to this planet, and I knew that this power could not be channeled by any individual, but only by a gathered body or bodies of people. I sensed that this force was meant to transform the consciousness on the planet and knew that the Pendle Hill conference had been shaped by this force.

On the Sunday morning of the conference, I was awakened early and found myself in a state of unusual clarity and peacefulness. It was the moment to stop struggling against knowing what God wanted from me. I looked at the various ways God was calling me to contribute to spiritual renewal among Friends, which I knew could be fulltime work. I saw how God wanted to use me to do this work, and I also saw that God wanted my meeting to support me in this. In that moment it was all quite simple and evident. "I must ask my meeting to release me," I thought, which I understood to mean that I must ask my meeting for support, including financial support, in order that I might be released from the obligation of doing work other than my ministry.

A Friend with whom I spoke after the conference encouraged me to be obedient. Clarity about this remained for several days, but then I was beset by doubts and fears. At Christmas I had a series of dreams that revealed requesting release from my meeting would lead to a painful process that somehow was a necessary part of fully becoming a member of the community.

I prayed and struggled, asking God why I couldn't just continue as I was, being self reliant by teaching part time and giving my free time to ministry? Finally one day I said to God, "Okay, God, I admit that my way has failed. Help me do things your way." After I said this I felt an astonishing rush of energy through me, a release of something that had been a tight knot inside me. After more laboring, I reached a sense of clarity and drafted a letter to my meeting. I took this letter to the woman who served as my spiritual companion; she encouraged me to send it.

Finally, I mailed the completed letter to the clerk of my meeting. Shortly after I arrived home from the post office, my longtime friend Kathryn Gordon called to tell me that at the October conference at Pendle Hill, she had a leading to give me $4000, money which she did not have at that time. I was struck by the synchronicity: I had received the leading to ask my meeting for support at the same gathering at which Kathryn received the leading to offer me money. At that time, however, I hadn't seen clear to obey this leading, nor had the money been available to Kathryn. At the very time I had acknowledged and obeyed my leading, the money had unexpectedly become available to Kathryn.

My immediate impulse was to decline her offer. On the other hand, the synchronicities were so uncanny that I knew I must pay attention to what God might be doing, for I had seen God work in my life through amazing synchronicities in the past. I asked her for time to discern about this.

In the meantime, my meeting considered my letter of request at our next business meeting. While some Friends expressed the thought that the request deserved serious consideration, others raised objections. The business meeting began a long and often difficult process of considering the request. Eventually a clearness committee was appointed which discerned that I was Spirit-led, but did not reach unity on what kind of support the meeting might give me. In the meantime, I understood that the meeting was not going to see clear to provide me with any financial support in the near future, if ever. This made me see Kathryn's leading in a new light.

I saw that to refuse her offer would be to impede God's work. I had to trust that God would provide for her as well as me. I accepted Kathryn's money, but even after receiving a check from her, I hesitated to cash it. I prayed about this and asked my spiritual companion to help me with discernment. With her help, I came to understand that Kathryn's opportunity to make a personal sacrifice to support my work was a way God was working with her. Then I experienced an immense gratitude that was accompanied by a sensation of an outpouring of blessings flowing out of my heart toward her.

It has been more than a year since I accepted Kathryn's gift. My life has changed radically. Not only did I leave college teaching, but I understood that I must do all that I could to release myself. I could no longer live by myself in my own apartment, but must live more economically, in community with others. I therefore joined a Quaker ministry in North Philadelphia, sharing a house in a low-income neighborhood with two other people. In another amazing synchronicity, Kathryn was simultaneously but independently led to move from New Paltz, New York, to join a different Quaker household in North Philadelphia. We now live about twelve blocks apart and gather weekly with other Friends for worship.

In April of this year, my meeting approved a minute of religious service recognizing that I was authentically called to ministry and expressing support for my work.

The money Kathryn gave me has been gone for months now, but in the meantime I've received unsolicited financial gifts, small and large, from friends and from my grandmother. Friends have also generously contributed in non-financial ways that have supported and enabled me to give as fully as possible of my time and energy to ministry among Friends. My task is to trust God and continue to remain open to divine guidance and teaching. I know more clearly than before that God is at work in the Society of Friends, transforming us into agents for important transformations in society, change that must begin within individuals. I know we are called to be a bold and prophetic witness to our world.

Marcelle Martin is a member of Chestnut Hill Friends Meeting (Pennsylvania), which has minuted her ministry of spiritual nurture. She teaches and leads retreats, and is the author of two Pendle Hill pamphlets: Invitation to a Deeper Communion *and* Holding One Another in the Light.

(*What Canst Thou Say?* August 1998 "Discernment")

~~~~~~~~~~~~~

The Four Thousand Dollars

Kathryn Gordon

I had known Marcelle for fifteen years, during which she had been first a graduate school classmate, then a friend, and finally a counselor and spiritual guide, who led me to heal from childhood trauma and open to the inner guide. It was God, I knew, who had guided me from depression to happiness, dysfunction to productivity, delusion to self-knowledge, atheism to Christ. But often I had thought that God could not have done it without Marcelle's love.

At the first Mysticism Among Friends Today conference, I began to feel moved to offer Marcelle financial support. Because I was, like her, trying to make my living teaching freshman composition courses as an adjunct, I knew how draining it could be. I was worried about her health. This concern weighed on me throughout the weekend.

At the last gathered meeting, I asked, "Should I offer Marcelle money, and if so how much?" Immediately a vein or artery just above my heart pulsed strongly four times. I felt this meant four thousand dollars. This seemed to me a clear answer to a clear question. I was grateful for the clarity but was now faced with a new problem: I did not have that much money.

That was October. Early in the new year, my sister Gail called me one day and said, "I'm about to mail you a check for five thousand dollars." This was a complete surprise; my portion of the expected sale of my mother's house, which Gail had decided, despite her own tight budget, to give me early. Here was the money meant for Marcelle. That same day I called Marcelle and offered her the four thousand dollars, telling her about the leading I had felt at the conference. She thanked me and said she would consider my offer. A letter from her arrived a few days later, informing me, "Synchronistically, your call came less than an hour after I mailed a letter to my meeting asking it to consider releasing me."

While I waited for the check and for Marcelle to decide whether or not to accept my offer, many doubts, fears, and temptations arose. I examined my motives. Was this a true leading or an attempt to gain approval? Was I actually afraid of success, and so divesting myself of money that could be used to undertake various projects I had planned? If Marcelle declined the money, would that mean my leading had been imagined?

I labored through this and much more. As days passed and I knew the check was coming in the mail, I began to give up responsibility for my leading; that is, while not consciously deciding to retract the offer, I started to tell myself that Marcelle was probably going to reject it in the end anyway. Temptation grew, and I recognized as I never had before certain feelings associated with going against one's conscience.

The check came and I deposited it. The teller invited me for a free investment advice session with a bank officer. As the banker talked, I began to think of the money as mine and to covet the interest and respect it could earn.

But then, as I was walking out of the bank, I distinctly heard the words, *It's not your money.* It's not your money. Never were four words more welcome! I was returned to the certainty I had felt at the first touch of the leading. Driving home, I rose from that certainty to a level of peaceful non-attachment, not just to the money but to the consequences of passing it on. I felt a humble joy—that I had followed my guidance and so danced the right steps at the right time.

I was not surprised when I arrived home, to hear Marcelle's voice on the answering machine. She had decided to accept the gift. My sister's check cleared on that same day, and on the next I mailed a check for four thousand dollars to the one person whom I knew, of a certainty, God wanted it to go.

(*What Canst Thou Say?* August 1998 "Discernment")

~ ~ ~ ~ ~ ~ ~ ~ ~ ~ ~ ~

Echoes from the Burning Bush

Traditional Gospel Song

Moses stood on holy ground;
Fire from God descended down;
Set the roadside bush on fire.
Then the Lord did there explain
To his servant should remain
All the echoes from the bush on fire.

All the echoes from this bush
How they thrill my soul;
All the echoes from this bush
Point me to my goal.

I ain't no more in doubting,
But with joy am shouting,
With no thoughts ashamed to blush;
This my song shall ever be,
Words that are so sweet to me,
Echoes from the burning bush.[31]

(*What Canst Thou Say?* November 2000 "Visions and Voices")

~ ~ ~ ~ ~ ~ ~ ~ ~ ~ ~ ~

A Time of Celebration

Mariellen Gilpin

My uncle Ralph Hall was a Presbyterian missionary to the cowboys of the Southwest. When he rode into a group of cowboys, he simply asked if they needed an extra hand. They always did, and for a few days he worked as hard as any of them. Cowboys lived and worked under brutalizing conditions, and were a hard-bitten lot. They frequently gave my uncle the meanest horse in the outfit to ride, and after he'd been bucked out of the saddle, he'd climb back on the horse and ride it the rest of the shift. (The horse's shift, that is. Cowboys didn't have shifts.) Then one evening he'd go to the foreman and explain he was a minister and would like to speak to the boys after supper. By that time, the cowboys respected Uncle Ralph as a man, and many lives were changed as a result of his ministry.

I grew up in Indiana and didn't meet Uncle Ralph until I was in college. My father was dying of cancer, and my aunt and uncle came from New Mexico on the train to help out during the last few weeks of my father's illness. I was very angry with my father, who was a compulsive gambler and had no medical insurance. I was also angry with my mother, who had kept my father in spite of his profligacy. I dropped out of college in order to help out with the farm chores and provide some financial support to my parents—I got a job in a men's prison. But when my father hadn't conveniently died before the start of the fall semester, I went back to college anyway. It was time to get on with my life. I was feeling singularly unlovely when Uncle Ralph walked into my life.

The first weekend after my aunt and uncle arrived, I drove home from college to meet them. When I arrived Uncle Ralph was doing the chores, so I changed into my barn clothes and went to see if I could help. Uncle Ralph was in the hog barn when I found him.

I saw him before he saw me. He was squatting to shell an ear of corn for some baby pigs to eat. I looked at the piggies. They were thriving on the corn, and also on the attention of the man who was feeding them. They knew Uncle Ralph liked them. I knew from my aunt that Uncle Ralph had never worked with pigs before, and I smiled at the incongruity of the cowboy boots and ten-gallon hat in an Indiana pigsty. I liked pigs, and I liked this man who wasn't too proud of being a cowboy to like them, too. Then I spoke, and Uncle Ralph looked up. He looked at me with love and joy, and I knew this man walked his talk—he was an authentic Christian.

All through the last days of my father's life, I watched Uncle Ralph and the atmosphere of love and joy that surrounded him. I wanted what he had. After we buried my father, I never saw my uncle and aunt again. I didn't write to them often, as I got married, became a Quaker, went to graduate school, and got a job. But I drew comfort knowing that Uncle Ralph was somewhere on this green planet with me.

Then Uncle Ralph died. I was again in a difficult time. My marriage was on hard times, and I had been let go from my job. I was unsure of my career direction, and had no job prospects. Again I was feeling unlovely. And now Uncle Ralph, who had been an anchor, was gone. I was short of cash; it was out of the question to travel halfway across the continent for his funeral. I decided to dedicate the next Sunday's worship to him. I would have my own private memorial meeting for worship.

When I mentioned to God that meeting for worship was for Uncle Ralph, I expected to cry. Suddenly there was a clear message: *And be assured, I am with you always.*[32] I realized Uncle Ralph wanted me to know he was quoting Jesus, and he also was speaking for himself. And there was that same atmosphere of love and joy I knew from the old days. I was deeply comforted.

A few weeks later my cousin wrote that Uncle Ralph had left instructions his funeral service was to be a celebration. And Uncle Ralph made sure my memorial meeting, too, was a time of celebration. I am deeply comforted.

Mariellen Gilpin is clerk of Urbana-Champaign Meeting, Illinois.

(*What Canst Thou Say?* August 2003 "Celebration and Thanksgiving")

~ ~ ~ ~ ~ ~ ~ ~ ~ ~ ~ ~

Hide

Mike Resman

So, who's going to explain?

They won't believe me
even if I am able to speak.

So I hope I never
collapse in public
from adoration of You.

My downcast eyes
hide
tears of joy
gathering in the corners.

I'm trying
to live
normal
in the world.

But it's getting so hard
when Love breaks through.

Mike Resman is a member of Rochester Friends Meeting (Minnesota).

(*What Canst Thou Say?* November 2001 "Kundalini Energy")

~ ~ ~ ~ ~ ~ ~ ~ ~ ~ ~ ~

Belize Park: From Dream to Reality

Judy Lumb

Barranco is a beautiful village on the coast in southern Belize. Sitting atop a fifteen-foot cliff above the black volcanic sand beach, one can see the mountains of Guatemala rising on the other side of the bay. I asked, "What is between here and the Sarstoon River, the southern border of Belize?" The answer came in Creole: "Lone bush." I thought, "What an opportunity for a national park!" Not two months later the Sarstoon-Temash National Park was declared, just as I had envisioned.

This is a story about being led, how one small step at a time was revealed to me. I had been invited to teach the Barranco Women's Craft Group to make quilts, but before I went, I was led to make some calls about a co-management project. Co-management of protected areas is my special interest, the intersection between the environment and the people. Belize is blessed with a wealth of natural resources, but the government does not have the resources to manage these areas. So, local people co-manage protected areas in partnership with the government.

I called government officials to see what their plans were for the Sarstoon-Temash National Park. Would they be receptive to a proposal for co-management? This park was surrounded by five indigenous villages—one Garifuna village on the coast, and four Kekchi villages in the rainforest. There were no other national parks co-managed by either culture. It seemed an excellent opportunity.

I inquired about funding such a project. This was unusually forward of me to make these calls. I was ill—mostly confined to hammock or bed—and I didn't get out much. I was able to use my computer from my hammock and published the *Belize Audubon Society Newsletter*, so I knew who to call.

I mentioned co-management of the park to the women as we worked on the quilts, but they were very focused on the sewing and did not respond to the park discussion. About six months later I got a letter saying, "Judy, you know that tourist thing you were talking about? You have to come back and help us write a proposal. A man came saying there was money." I responded that I would be there for the dügü in August.

That August was an incredible experience of being led. Before I caught the boat for Barranco, I was offered two indigenous language dictionaries and Bibles in the same languages. I didn't have enough money to buy the books, so I went to the bank and got a cash advance to cover the books and my expenses for the whole month. I had only planned to stay in Barranco a week and had not brought much money, but this small exchange made it possible for me to follow the leadings that were to come in Barranco for the rest of the month.

A *dügü* was a week-long family healing ceremony that was profoundly spiritual. The Garifuna people were devout Catholics, and their traditional culture was intertwined with their Catholic religion. Both a Catholic priest and a traditional priest officiated in an atmosphere of spiritual depth that opened my heart to be led. In the midst of all the Masses, drumming and dancing, small, incremental steps were revealed to me a little at a time over the entire week:

"You should come and stay in Barranco for a month to study the Garifuna language."

"Next February would be a good time to do that.*"*

"There should be a gathering in Barranco of the five villages surrounding the park to discuss co-management."

"I can't organize a workshop, but in February Rob Horwich (an expert on co-management) will be in Belize to help.*"*

"You should visit the four Kekchi villages."

"But wait a minute—I can barely walk! Barranco is only reachable by boat—there are no vehicles here. These villages are four, eight, and eleven miles away!*"*

"You can rent a horse."

"OK, I found a horse to rent, but there is no saddle.*"*

"Another family has a saddle."

I had just mentioned to my friend Shorty that I might visit the Kekchi villages when the Village Council Chair of one of those villages walked up—from four miles away!

After the dügü, we held a village meeting in Barranco to propose the idea of a gathering, and all agreed it was a good idea. Then I took a short walk with Shorty—four days, spending a day in each village. My horse was very slow and obstinate. It took Shorty pushing a wheelbarrow behind him to make him move. The fourth village was Crique Sarco; it was up the Temash River about 40 miles, so Shorty rented a boat. I asked the people in the villages if they would be interested in coming to a workshop in Barranco. They all were willing, but they didn't understand what a national park was. They thought I meant a football (soccer) field.

When I got home I made a few calls from my hammock and everything fell into place. I was chosen, not because I could do the work, but because I knew who to call. I got a promise of funding of the workshop, arranged for two facilitators who spoke both Garifuna and Kekchi, and got government officials to participate.

I had just written a short proposal and mailed it out when my father died. For several months I was not functional. It was the upcoming workshop that snapped me out of that depression.

By the end of the workshop, the communities had agreed to participate in this co-management project. They now have a large grant and are in the process of assessing the flora and fauna to develop a management plan.

While I still follow their progress, my role was only to bring the workshop into being. In retrospect I can see how all those individual leadings fit together—the book offering that led me to get enough money, the appearance of the Village Council Chair, the availability of a horse and saddle. I think it was only because of the spiritual depth of the dügü that my heart was opened enough to receive the messages. What else am I missing in my mundane daily life?

Judy Lumb *is a member of Atlanta Friends Meeting, but lives in Belize, Central America, where she edits, publishes, and writes.*

(*What Canst Thou Say?* May 2004 "Guidance")

~~~~~~~~~~~~~

Stretch out Your Hands

Maurine Pyle

For several years I rented a bedroom in my condominium to a boarder. Todd wasn't just any old boarder. I had met him at our Quaker meeting one Sunday morning where he had gone seeking solace for his troubles. Somehow his life got tangled up with mine. That is how God does it. A simple hello eventually leads to someone living in your back bedroom. What brought Todd eventually to my door was a deep desire for spiritual direction, something he had longed for all of his life. I became his guide and mentor for three years while he struggled.

One night at the dinner table as we were enjoying his good home cooking, I noticed that he was very sad, more sad than usual. When I inquired, he told me his friend Betty, an Internet buddy from Colorado, was quite ill with breast cancer. I suggested that we sit and pray for Betty after dinner.

As we centered into silence I immediately and clearly heard a word—*fragrance*. I held onto this word until our meditation had ended. I knew exactly where to go next—*Song of Songs*, Chapter I. Although I rarely touch this book of the Bible, I quickly found the verse I was looking for: *When your name is spoken aloud, it is like a spreading perfume.*[33] I told Todd that this was a message for Betty. He was used to my odd intuitive ways, so he immediately went to send her an email message. Her reply came in an instant:

"Bless Maurine. That quotation was cross-stitched by a friend of mine and sits framed on my mantle next to my children's pictures."

How did I know? I did not know. I am willing to bear a message and this one was stunningly specific. What did it mean? To me it meant God was sending a direct blessing to Betty to comfort her. I was simply the messenger.

In John 21:18 Jesus says to Peter, "I tell you solemnly as a young man, you fastened your belt and went about as you pleased. But when you are older you will stretch out your hands and another will tie you fast and carry you off against your will." Afterwards, Jesus said, "Follow me."

I first stretch out my hands and then I follow where I am led. That is how some miracles are worked.

Maurine Pyle, *Lake Forest Friends Meeting (Illinois) was servant leader, otherwise known as clerk, and is now Field Secretary, of Illinois Yearly Meeting.*

(*What Canst Thou Say?* May 2004 "Guidance")

~ ~ ~ ~ ~ ~ ~ ~ ~ ~ ~ ~ ~

Liking What I Have to Do

Carolyn Smith Treadway

My family was associated with the Conservative branch of Friends. It was at boarding school that meeting for worship came alive for me, because meeting for worship sometimes became an intense time of sharing in our beloved community. Why did a bald idea, not elegantly stated, strike me deeply at that time? It was this: "It's not doing what you like to do, but liking what you have to do, that makes life blessed." I realized decades later that the same basic message is carried in a poem by Tagore:

> *I slept, and dreamt that life was joy;*
> *I awoke, and found that life was duty;*
> *I acted, and behold: duty was joy.*

Involvement with my family, including five children, and a small career for fifteen years as City Clerk in our small town, sometimes left me feeling, "The only way out is through." I was able to keep doing what needed to be done—my duty as I saw it. Taking care of myself was part of that duty. Pierre Ceresole put it this way: "Never ask that circumstances become easier, but always that one's strength become greater, and joyfully accept rest and ease when they come along the way."

My only notable dark night of the soul experience, during a bout of insomnia at about age 35, put me at a great distance from Earth, showing me its insignificance. If the whole Earth is small, how much smaller was my life, my work. For years I read and consulted with anyone who might have knowledge of such things. The distilled result of my search:

Let go of everything.

Expect nothing.

Live in the moment.

With that frame of reference, the question becomes: what should one do? This needs to be answered day by day, hour by hour. We have chosen to live in a family compound with children and grandchildren, which means whatever we do is balanced against needs at home.

I do not know if the birth to me personally of a child with a disability would have devastated me. I am taking my cue from our daughter and son-in-law, who were somehow ready for it. A few months before Philip's birth, they met a Downs syndrome baby. They said if God should give them such a child, they would welcome it joyfully. And so they have. I don't feel that Philip is any more broken than our children and other grandchildren (nine distinct individuals with challenges and problems). We have had worries about each of them, except for the youngest; no doubt she will come up against something sooner or later. In many ways, Philip is more predictable than any of the rest.

Philip is now an exuberant, music-loving boy, learning at six many things commonly learned at two or three. He explores the world boldly with a grandparent to shadow him and keep him from harm. Moving stones from the gravel driveway into a container or onto a piece of board fascinates him, while I sit within sight, occupied with equally fascinating activities such as crocheting or shelling beans.

I know that I exist, because I am conscious. I did not make myself. I am amazed to be here. The dust from which I come, and to which I shall return, is astonishing stuff. However far back one goes, to the hot stuff of the early universe, the potential is there for consciousness, for empathy, for appreciation of beauty, for love and suffering, for joy.

Carolyn Smith Treadway *is a member of Yellow Springs Friends Meeting (Ohio). Daily practice includes first-thing-in-the-morning stretching exercises, based partly on yoga. This is somewhat meditative, though neither more nor less so than washing dishes, sweeping the floor, picking beans, or walking.*

(What Canst Thou Say? August 2000

"Wholeness in the Midst of Brokenness")

Thank You, God, for All of It

Jennifer Elam

Where can I go from thy Spirit?
Or where can I flee from thy presence?
If I ascend into heaven, thou art there;
If I make my bed in hell, behold, thou are there.
If I take the wings of the morning,
And dwell in the uttermost parts of the sea,
Even there thy hand shall lead me.
If I say, "Surely the darkness shall fall on me,"
Even the night shall be light about me;
Indeed, the darkness shall not hide from thee.
But the night shines as the day;
The darkness and the light are both alike to thee.[34]

The Psalm, and my own experiences of darkness being turned into good, leave me with the prayer, "Thank you, God, for all of it." In trying to understand my own experiences of God, I listened to the stories of many others. Those stories ranged from experiences of awe at the beauty of God in nature, to experiences of God that were so intense and overwhelming that the person ended up with a diagnosis of mental illness. They had experiences for which they could not find frameworks or integrate positively until much later. Annie told me as she opened to God, she was also opened to early trauma. A similar experience happened to Jane following a prayer for complete healing. They both said to me their symptoms were part of the healing process. I was dumbfounded, taken aback, and asked, "Why, if this is a healing process, is it called an illness?" I don't yet know the answer to my own question, but this questioning has led me to the realization of the possibility of God working through anything. It has been liberating. I know that I can do my best and God will work through me.

Many others have said to me that they can see clearly in retrospect that their hearts were hardened and had to be broken open so they could be transformed toward growing in God. Like David in the Psalms, it has come clear to me that God is available to transform even the darkest night to Light and use it.

For about three weeks in 1993, I was unable to feel God's presence in my life. It was the first time it had happened. I felt alienated and isolated from people as well as God. The words that best describe the feeling are the Biblical descriptions of hell. Yet, today I look back and see that I learned more from that experience than any other in my life. It taught me new levels of compassion.

It was in that moment I knew myself capable of any evils known to mankind. I knew I was no better than anyone else, and it was only by grace that I led a gifted life. It was a moment that gave me a glimpse of Divine compassion. I seek to live a life of compassion. Years of uncertainty about how that looks in the world have followed, but I am committed to listen and to live on the path where God has set me.

I know that God can take any experience and any mistake I make, and turn it into good. I am grateful for all of life that comes my way—and am often unable to see the gift in the moment. It takes all of it for the richness and wholeness to emerge.

Jennifer Elam is a member of Berea Meeting, Kentucky, a psychologist, and has written a book, Dancing with God through the Storm: Mysticism and Mental Illness, *which can be ordered from <jenelam@aol.com>.*

(*What Canst Thou Say?* August 2003 "Celebration and Thanksgiving")

~~~~~~~~~~~~~

Opting to Live

Carol Roth

I have decided to opt to live. For a while there I let myself get so tired of the pain that I really became depressed. Having had experiences wherein I went to other levels and knew of the peace and beauty that awaits, I began to yearn to go home where pain would be gone. But something happened this past week that has turned my entire thought system around. What I am going to relate is just an incident but boy, what it did to my soul is amazing.

On a very windy day last week our overhead gutters were clogged with leaves, and I wanted to spare my mailman hubby, Martin, more work. After surgery on my shoulder I couldn't move my arm to use the wire brush to sweep out the gutters, so I asked my daughter Morgan to help.

Morgan is 20 and lives at home while attending college. She was born with what are called essential tremors. Fine tremors run though her body, especially her hands, constantly. She is also a tiny little slip of a girl, weighing at the most ninety pounds. We got out the ladder and since I couldn't sweep out the gutters, Morgan got onto the top rung of the ladder. My role was to stay under her, holding onto her legs, which were shaking just as much from the cold wind as from her tremors.

We did the entire back of the house. We moved around to a one-foot section on the side where the drainspout came out of the gutter. In only a moment we would be done, back into a warm house for lunch and hot tea. I said to Morgan as I looked up at her, "Be careful, honey. Don't let the wire brush fall into the drainspout." A second later came the thunkety-thunk of the long-handled wire brush going down the drainspout.

She looked down at me, her eyes wide with disbelief. I helped her down off the ladder, where we both collapsed in laughter, sitting on the cold ground, just hugging each other, laughing like crazy. I bet we sat there for fifteen minutes, hugging and laughing.

We knew we had to get the wire brush out from where it was stuck in the curve of the drainspout as it neared the pavement. But how? It was a stiff wire brush with a very long handle. The curved end of the drainspout was riveted together, not screwed or bolted. If we left the brush in, the spout could be clogged with ice come winter.

I asked Morgan to unwind the hose and drain the water out. I had the idea that the hose would be flexible enough when free of water. I would put it in the drainspout underneath the brush and push the darn thing straight up until the brush popped out of the top.

Morgan drained the hose and brought it over to me. So I took the hose in hand and stuck my right hand in the spout with the hose.

Good. There were the stiff bristles of the wire brush. This would so easy....

My hand got caught. It was caught in between the wire brush and the hose. I tried to slide it out. No way. The wire bristles were cutting into it. The hose was up against my hand, and there was no way to get my hand out. Morgan said, "Mom, what's wrong?" I replied, "My hand is stuck. It is really, really stuck. I can't get my hand out."

She plopped down next to me. We looked at each other and started to laugh again. We howled, we giggled, we laughed and laughed. The wind was fierce and we were so cold and yet, I was so happy because I felt so grounded in the sense of the moment we were caught in. My daughter's eyes were beautiful, her laughter so rich and full. The wind was delicious. I was fully human, fully alive, totally in tune with the earth, with the soul beside me. I wasn't thinking of being far away from pain, of leaving the earth. I was filled with love for where I was, who I was as a human being, and I knew that I wanted more— more laughter, more interactions with others. I wanted the insane moments, the silly moments. I wanted to feel the cold, the wind against my face. I wanted to be here when Morgan graduates. I wanted to live...

I asked Morgan to go into the house and call 911. We needed help. She wanted to know what to say and I said, "Just tell them that your mom has her hand caught up in the drainspout. We'll take the police, a plumber, just send some help." Morgan was aghast. "Oh, Mom, just keep trying to free your hand, just try once more."

I did. And it worked. I managed to ease my scraped hand out, pushed the hose against the wire brush and there it went; the brush popped out of the top of the rainspout. We did it! Success. Hugging, laughing, now exhausted, we entered the house.

When the wire brush flew upwards out of the top of the drainspout, it was as though something that was clogged inside of my own soul simply burst through as well. This seems so silly. But it was a turning point for me. I opt to live. There is such conviction in me now. I have chosen to live; I will live with full attention and full awareness of the time I have to spend here. I will live in attention, in awareness, in appreciation that I am just as human as I am spiritual. I will work to help the healers help me, and I will do the best I can to live a life of humor and awe.

Carol Roth *was a member of the* WCTS *editorial team in the 1990s. She sent us this report on how the Spirit is finding her as she lives with a chronic illness.*

(*What Canst Thou Say?* February 2001
"The Spirit in Quaker Business Practice")

~ ~ ~ ~ ~ ~ ~ ~ ~ ~ ~ ~ ~

> *Let all the strains of joy mingle in my last song—*
> *The joy that makes the earth flow over*
> *In the riotous excess of the grass;*
> *The joy that sets the twin brothers, life and death,*
> *Dancing over the wide world,*
> *Shaking, and the joy that sweeps in with the tempest,*
> *Waking all life with laughter...*
> *The joy that sits still with its tears*
> *On the open red lotus of pain,*
> *And the joy that throws everything it has*
> *Upon the dust, and knows not a word.*[35]

—Rabindranath Tagore (1861–1941)

(*What Canst Thou Say?* May 1998 "Healing")

Afterword: God as Companion

Mariellen Gilpin

The stories in this book reveal some of the faces of God: redeemer, parent, lover, teacher, guide. Most of all, however, the stories reveal a God who desires to be friend and companion—listener, supporter, counselor, giver of gifts—constant in love, forgiving of mistakes, respecter of our right to decide for ourselves what to do. The God in these stories walks closely with us in the challenges and joys of life on earth.

For God to become friend and companion, we have to become friends and companions of God. It feels presumptuous at first to think of ourselves as friends of the Creator of the universe, but how can we expect God to be our friend if we are not willing to be friends of God? How do we become friends of God? We can look at our most growthful human friendships to learn about being a friend of God. A friendship that helps us grow is our truest friendship, and can tell us the most about friendship with God.

True friends listen to one another. A true friend lets us complain when we need to, before we can even begin to focus on problem-solving. God listens to our prayers, and we must learn to listen to God. The stories in this book show that God may break into our awareness at any time, but it helps if we are listening. Linda Theresa ("In the Heart of Pain") becomes open to listening for God when she is totally immersed in chronic unending pain; when she listens, pain becomes a gift. It is time to turn off the radio and television, and seek God's presence through loving attention to the life around us, and to the silence at the core of the universe.

True friends seek each other's company. They hang out together. The people in these stories make opportunities to be with God regularly, to talk, of course, but also simply to *be* together. Amy Perry goes into the desert ("This

Desert Land") in order to be with God, and the mountains and yucca speak of God. We can wash the supper dishes mindfully; when we are totally in the moment, we are in the presence of God. As ordinary people we can become whole when we regularly seek the presence of God.

True friends care for each other enough to ask the hard questions. Mutual asking of hard questions binds the relationship. The people in these stories haven't hesitated to question God. We may wish God ran the universe more to our liking: why does there have to be sorrow, pain and disability, loneliness, war or terror? Dimitri Mihalas ("Depression is a Gift") goes through frightening depression and asks, "Why?" But he finds the presence of God in the depth of despair, and learns it is in deepest darkness that we can most easily see light. In "Praying for Problem People" Lauren Leach has a temper tantrum when God doesn't answer her prayers as she wishes. When God's answer becomes clear, she realizes it was in front of her the whole time. She is the one who was blind and deaf, not God. God challenges us to face our fears, our mistakes, our faults and maladjustments, our desire for easy answers to hard questions. God wants us to work hard at changing because God loves us.

True friends give each other space. When we ask that hard question, we don't expect an answer immediately. We let our friend think it over. When the friends of God ask their burning questions, they wait for the answer to bubble forth like a fountain out of mutual silence. In "The Gift That Follows Surrender" David Blair thinks he wants only to apologize to his former friend, but God says "*No.*" Then David surrenders all desire to control the outcome to meet his own desires, and God gives the opportunity to apologize. God gives us space, and we must reciprocate. God's answer will appear in God's time, and in God's way.

True friends do things for each other. When our friend is laid up with two sprained ankles, we don't hesitate to shop for groceries. These stories remind us that God does for us by giving us summer and winter, sun and rain, everything in its season. We for our part are called to do for God: work in the soup kitchen, choose the job that helps others instead of the job that will make us rich in things, wipe the tears of the oppressed, speak truth to the oppressor. We can be God's companions in the work of the world. In "A Deer Shall Lead Thee" Hazel Jonjak got rid of her Bronco because driving it five miles to work made her complicit in the killing in Iraq. It wasn't easy, but serving God brought serenity in the face of inconvenience.

True friends trust each other. They tell each other the hard stuff, and they support one another. In "Go to Camp David" God entrusted Stephen Angell with an errand, and Steve trusted enough to do what God asked. God may ask us to break a bad habit. We trust God when we choose to ignore our strong negative feelings and break the bad habit, one hard decision at a time, until the new pattern of choice emerges. We can trust God to be with us while we fearfully respond to the same old stimulus in a new way. We may fear changing our bad old way—we don't like its effects, but we do know what to expect. There is security in knowing what will happen, even when we know it will be painful. In correcting an old mistake, we fear making fresh new mistakes. We can trust God to help us learn new and better ways.

Not only do the stories in *Discovering God as Companion* reveal God's desire to be our friend and companion, they tell us God is still active, just as the prophets said. God has not stopped speaking to us just because Jesus and the apostles no longer walk the earth. We discover revelation is ongoing, rather than frozen in some past time and place. The same Spirit that animated the writers of the gospels is available to us today. We have no more important task than to listen for God's ongoing revelation in today's world—today's issues and concerns—in the lives of God's children here and now.

How are we to listen for God's presence in our lives? In "Focusing on the Experience" Ken Tapp spends time in nature, camera in hand. Nature heals his spirit, leaving him freer to hear God's voice. We can make an appointment with God, writing it in our datebooks if need be, setting aside time for prayer and worship. We can pray while we commute to work, put the clothes in the dryer, cut up the beans for cooking. We can talk to God in our own words, about our own concerns; often God will suggest things in our minds, making prayer an intimate conversation with one who loves us. We can read the Bible and other great spiritual literature, and we can ponder the meaning of what we read. We can talk about the things of God with friends who want to make God an important part of their lives. We can stop being busy, leaving time and silence so God can get a word in edgewise.

What If It's Not Real?

Powerful spiritual experiences may be disorienting. Jesus was tempted in the wilderness after his baptism by John. All of us have to work hard to choose positive actions and thoughts in the face of strong negative feelings. The mystic often has to try harder to discern the difference between his or her own self-will and a true experience of God. How can we respond wisely in the face of a mystical experience? How can we be helped to a right conclusion about the genuineness of a leading, whether it be from God or not? Here are a few guidelines:

You shall recognize them by the fruits they bear.[36] Jesus' advice can be applied not only to judging human spiritual leaders, but also to our inner experiences of being led. Does our mystical experience unhinge our minds and disorganize our lives? Does it encourage us to isolate from human contact, from rubbing up against reality? If we skip work in order to listen to God, it wasn't God's idea. A spiritual experience can start out sounding pretty good, but if it leads to greater and greater disintegration, it's not God at work. A voice that encourages us to behave in ways that unhinge our minds or do others harm comes from within us, not from God.

Every kingdom that is divided against itself goes to ruin.[37] In "Deciding Not to Pray," Mariellen Gilpin realizes the powers of darkness would not lead us to do good in order to bring us to some bad end. Conversely, God would not inspire us to do evil to bring about good. If it is clear to us that what we are about to say or do will bring comfort and help to someone in genuine need, it is probably God who is inspiring us.

Does this spiritual experience fit with the best Scripture has to offer about the character and motivations of God? If we are told to forgive, to remember God loves the person we're angry with at least as much as God loves us, God is speaking. A true experience will lead us to care for the welfare of the people around us and reach out to others in ordinary ways. God has work for us, work that ties us to people, to reality, to God's kingdom. When Theodora Waring ("Baptized by the Holy Spirit") has an experience in which she is known completely and loved, she feels called to share that love with others by becoming a hospital chaplain.

Does this spiritual leading meet the test of common sense? The real God brings common sense to our dilemma and encourages us to apply our own good sense before we act. A true mystical moment will often present food for thought rather than answers. God doesn't present a truckload of information, instead expecting us to think things through and come to our own conclusion. And God presents Light for the next step, not for the whole journey. Elizabeth Meyer ("The Nominating Voice") tests her voice over several months, in several different ways, before accepting the position of presiding clerk of her Friends meeting.

What do trusted friends think? We can check with people who know our weaknesses and are deeply committed to helping us think it through and decide what God wants us to do. Wise human friends and good counselors can present us with the word of the true God. Elaine Emily ("Interview with a Quaker Healer") has guided many to wholeness in the midst of intense spiritual experiences.

Testing Our Leadings in Solitude

Some leadings are best discerned in company; others in our own closet. In solitude we can proceed along these lines:

Pray for guidance. I think out loud in the presence of God: "Lord, I just heard a voice suggesting my desire is really true. I'm scared to death, and I'm also very attracted. Help me, please, sort inner demons from outer Truth." In "New Eyes" Connie Lezenby, for her part, has learned over and over there is a patient, wonderful waiting until she invites God to come closer. God is never invasive.

Reflect in the presence of God on what God may want me to do: "God, something in me wants my desire to be true. I want it so much I'm afraid I'm telling myself what I want to hear. Have I made it all up? It won't do me any good to separate myself from the Truth." In "Salt Doll" Kathy Tapp feels her spiritual experiences are distracting her from her spiritual practice. One day she understands that, conversely, her spiritual experiences *are* her spiritual practice.

Ask for what we need: "God, I still need at some very deep level for my desire to be true. Help me live with the essential mystery of things. Help me live with knowing I will never know. Help me let go of needing my desire to be true." Kat Griffith ("My Cup Runneth Over") knows she will never be able to stop yelling at her daughter without God's help. And when she asks, help is given.

Wait and see if it goes away. A true leading will continue to present itself to us over time, in many ways, and in several different contexts. We will come to see that our leading is a force for healing—or it will fade out of our consciousness.

Following Our Leadings

Sometimes—sometimes—the voice still seems to be reality after we try to think things through in God's presence. That voice helps us see our dilemma more objectively, and greater objectivity brings better thinking and better decision making. We want to hear that voice. How can we make it come to us more and more? God is present all the time; we're the ones not present to God. We can pray for help listening for God's presence. And we must continually test the guidance the voice presents. No one should hesitate to test whether the voice is that of God; God is a great deal more comfortable with careful examination than some of God's followers seem to think. "Life is complex, and there is no substitute for intelligence."[38] Here are three guidelines for testing leadings.

Take one small step—the smallest possible step—and observe the results. Does a way open? How do things work out? Then take the next smallest possible step, and again see whether reality intervenes or cooperates. It's a kind of inner scientific experimentation. In "Giving Birth to the Sun" Marcelle

Martin finds her way out of a life-and-death inner crisis by testing her leading carefully over many months. There can be many small steps before it becomes clear the call is indeed from God.

Step out in faith. If a way has repeatedly opened when I experiment with reality, I commit to a plan of action. There is nothing so powerful for increasing God's active guidance in our lives than doing what God asks of us, no matter how small the obedience asked. God told Stephen Angell ("Go to Camp David") whether to turn right or left before giving him a message for the President. If we are faithful in small matters, more will be given.

Try to learn from mistakes. Even when I am right about what God wants, I will need to make many mid-course corrections. Again, it's like scientific research. A mistake is not the end of the world. It is data we can learn from. When a job opens up and we apply, we may not be promoted. What can we learn from it? When God shuts one door, we can watch for another door to open somewhere else. In "Enraptured by Silence" Alvin Joaquin Figueroa thinks God doesn't want him to become a priest because Alvin doesn't measure up to God's standards, but slowly learns God has another even more fulfilling role for him. We can try to follow God's guidance as best we can, checking our outer experience against our inner at each step. It's not easy. But the smooth road of following our self-will never gets us where we want to go, so we learn to choose the rough road of watching for God's guidance and following where God leads.

In science, learning a new truth always introduces a new question. There is ever more to learn, and the authors in this book are always learning during their journeys to become friends and companions of God. As we try things, observe the results, step out in faith, and learn from our mistakes in our relationship with God, we can come to a new place, where we affirm this life—all of it—as a journey to God. Jennifer Elam writes, "Thank you, God, for all of it."

Ours is a journey in which—no matter how many or how terrible our mistakes, no matter how far off the true path we wander—we never have to beat through the underbrush to find our path again. Our path to God is always at our feet, waiting for us to make a better choice, to resume our journey to God. It's all God, and it's all data and all process: God is waiting for us wherever we wander, ready to help us try things, observe, step out in faith, learn, and turn to God once again. God is just as ready to be friend and companion when we are up to our armpits in the sticky mud of bad habits as God would be if we were standing on a mountain beneath a cloudless sky. God thinks our lives are too important to wait for us to get perfect before becoming our friend and companion. None of the writers in this book are extraordinarily saintly.

They're not done. They are all ordinary men and women who have done and heard and seen extraordinary things because they found themselves becoming friends and companions of God.

In our culture, someone who has mystical experiences feels alone; the church often is not prepared to help; and the mental health community often labels the individual mentally ill. In such a culture, *Discovering God as Companion* can be the beginning of a support group in print for those with mystical experiences. We can help one another up with a tender hand, encouraging and cautioning one another when needed.

This book contains the stories of real people, dealing with situations we have all faced, but dealing with them in awareness of the presence of God. The writers tell their stories because their experiences changed them—made them more whole—and they hope their readers change as well. We invite you to read, and ponder, and make your own experiments in the presence of God. It's all God, all data, and all process. Make your mistakes, your experiments, your invitations to God, boldly yet humbly. God is waiting.

Questions for Discussion

Below are some questions for an eight-session book study group. These questions invite participants to speak of their own spiritual experiences. Because these experiences are tender and difficult to put into words, it will be helpful to begin by developing groundrules for your group that create a zone of safety and of care for one another. For example, you may agree to simply receive one another's sharing but to avoid probing questions or evaluative comments. Or you may agree to keep the sharing confidential. Or you may decide to begin and end your time together with a period of prayer or of quiet.

Introductory Session

What has drawn you to this book? What interests you in reading the stories of people's experiences of God at work in their lives? How have you experienced movements of the Divine in your own life?

God Breaking In

Which of the stories in "God Breaking In" do you relate most fully to? What was it that struck you? How does the story resonate with your own experience? If any of the stories makes you think, "thanks but no thanks," what do you find off-putting? Have any of these stories expanded your concept of what to expect of God?

God in Nature

Did any of the stories in this section resonate with something in your own experience of awe or wonder in nature? Did your experience come to you in something small, like a grasshopper on a leaf, or in something larger, like a dramatic sunset? How have you looked at nature differently after your experience? Have you looked at God differently since?

God in Times of Pain and Despair

Has God ever spoken to you when, as Meister Eckhart said, you were "helpless and poverty-stricken?" What happened? What difference has your experience made in your life—do you think or feel or behave differently because of your experience? Did any of the stories in this section challenge you or your understanding of God? Did you draw comfort from one story in particular? What life lessons in these stories, or in the stories shared in the group, seem especially significant to you?

Living Faithfully

Paul Lacey has said, "We can be directed, daily, in what we do, the jobs we hold, the very words we say." How have you experienced that direction in your life? Do you follow any spiritual disciplines that help you be attuned to that source of direction? What do you do to lead a Spirit-led life? Have you ever been asked to step out in faith, and if so, what was that like? P.T. Forsythe says that prayer is like scientific experimentation. Have you ever experimented in prayer, and how did your experiment work out?

In Celebration

Jennifer Elam writes, "Thank you, God, for all of it." Has there been a significant challenge in your life that much later you have come to see as a gift from God? What was the challenge, and the gift? Have you had times when you were overflowing with joy for your life, just as it was, flaws and all? What has brought you to a sense of love, wonder, peace, and grace?

Afterword

In your own experience, has God been your friend and companion? How have you seen God's friendship and companionship in your life? What has been your most significant challenge to your becoming God's friend in your turn? The Afterword proposes several guidelines for testing an experience to decide whether it is self-will or God's will. How would you apply those tests to your own spiritual experiences? Can you add other tests to those suggested? Do some of the author's tests seem more useful in your experience than others she suggests?

Closing Session

Which story or stories speak to you most deeply in this book? What do you hope to do differently as a result of reading these stories? What do you need to do so that you can live differently—has a new spiritual practice suggested itself in the experiences shared by these writers? What has helped you do things differently in the past?

Who Are Friends (Quakers)?

The Religious Society of Friends, commonly known as Quakers, was founded in England in the 17th century. We are one of the historic "peace churches." We believe God is available to all people, without intermediaries (such as, for instance, a pastor or sacrament). Founder George Fox expressed it this way: *Christ has come to teach his people himself.* Friends speak of "that of God in everyone," "Inner Light," "Inward Christ," "the Spirit of Christ Within," and other phrases. We believe everyone has this seed of God, and Quakers try to hear what the Inward Guide is saying to us.

Quakerism is a mystical religion, but it differs from other mystical religions in two ways: First, our goal is not personal enlightenment so much as a communal search for God's will. Second, we do not withdraw from the world but instead translate our mysticism into action. Calls of the Spirit to action, as for instance, when Friends unanimously agreed not to hold slaves as early as the 1700s, can transform an individual, his or her meeting, the Society of Friends, or the whole society. Public eduation resulted from Friends' efforts toward equalizing society.

Quakers all believe in the necessity of being continually guided by the Light Within. Divine revelation is not restricted to the Bible, but continues today. God is available here and now, right where we are. We have a common core of *testimonies*, or shared perspectives on the world: peace, integrity, equality, and simplicity.

The Peace Testimony. Friends believe that it is wrong to use violence to solve problems. Many Quakers are conscientious objectors, advocates of nonviolence, and peace activists. American and British Quaker service organizations received the Nobel Peace Prize in 1947 for Friends' work in Europe during and after World War II.

The Testimony of Integrity. Friends place God at the center of their lives. Integrity is choosing to follow the leadings of the Spirit despite challenges from such sources as the desire for possessions or the regard of others. Speaking truth is a core value for Quakers. Friends accept responsibility for their actions.

The Testimony of Equality. Friends believe all people are created equal in the eyes of God. Friends were among the first to value women in the ministry and in the campaign for women's rights. Quakers were leaders in the anti-slavery movement, and pioneered humane treatment for prisoners and the mentally ill.

The Testimony of Simplicity. Friends prefer to own and use only what we need and avoid luxuries in order to avoid distractions from living in such a way as to hear and follow divine leadings.

We have no creed. There is a wide range of beliefs among Friends, and discovering what it truly means to be a Quaker means struggling with the differing viewpoints. Quaker faith has Christian roots, but Friends in the silent "unprogrammed" tradition may be fed spiritually by many spiritual traditions.

We have no special holidays, sacraments, or rituals, believing all of life is sacred. Weddings are performed by the wedding couple standing in the midst of a Meeting for Worship and speaking their vows to each other, in the presence of God, Friends, friends, and family.

Friends in the tradition of silent worship have no pastor. We gather in silent, expectant waiting to be moved by God to speak. When a member feels led to share a message, he or she speaks out of the silence. Messages are not prepared beforehand. Generally worship lasts about an hour. A first-time attender at a Friends meeting for worship explained it this way:

"I sat in silent worship my first Sunday, eagerly waiting for someone to be moved by God. What would it be like? What would the person say? The silence was restless at first as people settled into their seats. Then, quite suddenly, the silence deepened. Time deepened somehow, too. We waited in the silence. A man across the room stood up. It really was happening! God had selected someone and given him a message! He was brief: 'I have learned that prayer and scientific experiments are the same in method if not in concept.' He sat down. The miracle had happened.

"I grappled with the speaker's few words in ways that never happened during sermons. In the silence I thought, 'If prayer is like a scientific experiment, that means we're supposed to try things when we pray, and observe the results. It means we make mistakes. But it's okay to make mistakes if we learn from them. Are we supposed to form hypotheses about how to pray, and then pray that way, and see what happens? Does that mean there's no one right way to pray?' Then someone shook hands, and worship was over."

For more information about the Religious Society of Friends see <quaker. org>. To find a Quaker meeting near you go to <quakerfinder. org>. If reading *Discovering God as Companion* has nourished you for your spiritual journey, you can continue the conversation by subscribing and contributing your stories to *What Canst Thou Say?*. For more information go to <whatcanstthousay. org> or write to WCTS, 1035 Hereford Drive, Blue Bell PA 19422-1925.

Endnotes

All websites indicated below were accessed November 15, 2006.

[1] Dorothee Soelle, 2001. *The Silent Cry: Mysticism and Resistance.* Minneapolis: Fortress Press, p. 302.

[2] Rufus Jones, 1932. "Why I enroll with the mystics." In Vergilius Ferm, ed. *Contemporary American Theology*, Vol. 1, pp. 206–207.

[3] George Fox, *Journal of George Fox*, rev. ed., John L. Nickalls, ed., 1975. London: Religious Society of Friends, p. 22

[4] Philip St. Romain, 1991. *Kundalini Energy and Christian Spirituality.* New York: The Crossroad Publishing Company.

[5] Yvonne Kason, 1994. *A Farther Shore*. Toronto: HarperCollins.

[6] John Woolman, *The Journal and Essays of John Woolman*, Amelia Mott Gummere, ed., 1922. New York: The Macmillan Company, p. 58.

[7] Gurudev Shree Chitrabhanu, 1979. *The Psychology of Enlightenment: Meditations on the Seven Energy Centers*, Berkeley, CA: Asian Humanities Press, p, xv.

[8] Thomas Kelly, 1941. *A Testament of Devotion*, New York and London: Harper Brothers, p. 56.

[9] Thomas Berry, 1988. *The Dream of the Earth*, San Francisco: Sierra Club Books, p. 176.

[10] Psalm 118:24.

[11] Rachel Davis DuBois, in Philadelphia Yearly Meeting, 1997. *Faith and Practice,* Philadelphia, PA, p. 137, #173.

[12] Scott Russell Sanders, 1995. *Writing from the Center*, Bloomington and Indianapolis, Indiana: Indiana University Press, p. 168.

[13] This quotation is attributed to Meister Eckhart, but we have been unable to verify its origin.

[14] Caroline Fox, in Philadelphia Yearly Meeting, 1997. *Faith and Practice,* Philadelphia, PA, p. 131, #155.

[15] Mary Baker Eddy, 1994. *Science and Health: With Key to the Scriptures*, Boston, MA: First Church of Christ, Scientist, The Christian Science Board of Directors.

[16] Jennifer Faulkner, in Philadelphia Yearly Meeting, 1997. *Faith and Practice,* Philadelphia, PA, p. 134, #163.

[17] This quotation is attributed to Meister Eckhart, but we have been unable to verify its origin.

[18] Elizabeth Gray Vining, in Philadelphia Yearly Meeting, 1997. *Faith and Practice,* Philadelphia, PA, p. 111, #90.

[19] Matthew 12:25.

[20] Matthew 7:16.

21 Paul Lacey, 1985. *"On Leading and Being Led,"* *Pendle Hill Pamphlet #264,* Wallingford, Pennsylvania: Pendle Hill Publications, p. 3.

22 Isaac Penington, excerpts from letters to Catherine Pordage (letter 65, Sixth Month 1671), to Catherine Pordage and another (letter 66, Seventh Month 1671), and to Dulcibella Laiton (letter 83, Fifth Month 1677), Glenside, Pennsylvania: Quaker Heritage Press <qhpress.org/texts/penington>.

23 Teresa of Avila, *Interior Castle,* translated and edited by E. Allison Peers, 1989. New York: Image Books, Doubleday, p. 76.

24 George Fox, in Philadelphia Yearly Meeting, 1997. *Faith and Practice,* Philadelphia, PA, p. 171, # 285.

25 Deborah Haines, 1978, in Philadelphia Yearly Meeting, 1997. *Faith and Practice,* Philadelphia, PA, p. 151, # 213.

26 P.T. Forsythe, 1916. *The Soul of Prayer,* Grand Rapids, Michigan: William B. Eerdmans Publishing Company, Chapter VI, part two <spiritofprayer.com/soul01. php>.

27 Carolyn W. Treadway, 2001. "The Journey Home," and the concluding chapter of *Out of the Silence: Quaker Perspectives on Pastoral Care and Counseling,* J. William Ratliff, ed. Wallingford, Pennsylvania: Pendle Hill Publications.

28 This quotation is attributed to Meister Eckhart, but we have been unable to verify its origin.

29 Thomas Kelley, 1941. *A Testament of Devotion,* New York and London, Harper Brothers Publishers, pp. 56–61.

30 James Nayler, "From a transcript of Nayler's examination in trial at Appleby, 1652, on a charge of blasphemy," *Selections from the Writings of James Nayler,* Brian Drayton, ed., 1994. New England Yearly Meeting, Mosher Book and Tract Committee, p. 14.

31 Words and Music: Bryon Foust & V. O. Summar, 1943. On AcaDisc. #6: *Let Me Tell You about Jesus* by the Sounds of Glory. James D. Vaughan, Music Publisher, 1970. <acadisc.com/letme.htm#echoes >

32 Matthew 28:20.

33 Song of Songs 1:3.

34 Psalm 139:7–12.

35 Rabindranath Tagore, 1912. *Gitanjali (Song Offerings).* <etext.virginia.edu/toc/ modeng/public/TagGita.htm>

36 Matthew 7:16

37 Matthew 12:25

38 GROW, 1957. *Program of Growth to Maturity,* rev. ed. 1996. Marrickville, Australia: Aussie Press.

Author Index

Past Issues of *What Canst Thou Say?*

Why Canst Thou Say? Is a newsletter in which Quakers share first-hand their mystical experiences and contemplative practice. The first fourteen issues were published from October 1994 through May 1997. Each issue featured a variety of topics. Beginning with issue 15 in August 1997, the publication became quarterly, with each issue focusing on a specific theme:

Letting Your Life Speak, August 1997 (15)

Support for the Journey, November 1997 (16)

Deepening Worship and Ministry, February 1998 (17)

Healing, May 1998 (18)

Discernment, August 1998 (19)

Mentors, Mentoring, November 1998 (20)

Nature, February 1999 (21)

Dreams, May 1999 (22)

Speaking Out About Our Mystical Experiences, August 1999 (23)

Mystical Experiences in Childhood, November 1999 (24)

Wholeness in the Midst of Brokenness, February 2000 (25)

Traditions that Feed My Soul, May 2000 (26)

Called to Intercessory Prayer, August 2000 (27)

Visions and Voices, November 2000 (28)

Experiencing the Spirit in Quaker Business Process, February 2001 (29)

Solitude, May 2001 (30)

Forgiving, August 2001 (31)

Kundalini Energy, November 2001 (32)

Spiritual Experience and the Outward Life, February 2002 (33)

The Arts and the Spirit, May 2002 (34)

God's Marvelous Workarounds, August 2002 (35)

Spiritual Metaphors, November 2002 (36)

Death and Dying, February 2003 (37)

Birth and Rebirth, May 2003 (38)

Celebration and Thanksgiving, August 2003 (39)

Spiritual Healing, November 2003 (40)

Open and Tender, February 2004 (41)

Guidance, May 2004 (42)

Knowings, August 2004 (43)

Darkness, November 2004 (44)

Loving God with Our Whole Being, February 2005 (45)

Spiritual Emergence(y), May 2005 (46)

Seeing, August 2005 (47)

God's Humor, November 2005 (48)

Touched by the Spirit, February 2006 (49)

Changed by Grace, May 2006 (50)

Jesus, August 2006 (51)

Evil, November 2006 (52)

To subscribe or purchase copies of back issues of *What Canst Thou Say?*, see <whatcanstthousay.org> or write to WCTS, 1035 Hereford Drive, Blue Bell PA 19422-1925.

Printed in the United States
84327LV00008B/231/A

9 781425 987701